FOnD

Sport Fish
of
Fresh Water

JOhnDon

FS Books:

Sportsman's Best: Inshore Fishing
Sportsman's Best: Offshore Fishing
Sportsman's Best: Snapper & Grouper
Sportsman's Best: Sailfish
Sportsman's Best: Redfish

Sport Fish of Florida
Sport Fish of the Gulf of Mexico
Sport Fish of the Atlantic
Sport Fish of Fresh Water
Sport Fish of the Pacific

Baits, Rigs & Tackle
Annual Fishing Planner
The Angler's Cookbook

Florida Sportsman Magazine
Shallow Water Angler Magazine
Florida Sportsman Fishing Charts
Lawsticks
Law Boatstickers

Edited by Florida Sportsman and In-Fisherman Staff
Art Direction by Ron Romano and Jim Henderson
Copy Edited by Jerry McBride

ISBN 0-936240-23-7

Sport Fish
of
Fresh Water

By Vic Dunaway

Original Illustrations by
Kevin R. Brant

www.floridasportsman.com

www.in-fisherman.com

CONTENTS

Preface

The Nature of Fishing

For thousands of years before these times, men and women hunted, fished and gathered. These ancestors lived this way mainly as a matter of survival, though paintings on cave walls show that they celebrated and surely enjoyed their wildlife encounters.

Times have changed, but not that much the basic nature of fishing. The spark to seek, to understand, to interact with the natural world still burns within us. Of course, many of us fish for the table, because fish are both nutritious and delicious.

But we fish for sport, too, for fishing is a challenge. We puzzle over that which we can't easily see or touch through a water barrier. We seek to connect with this puzzle, these fish, with hook and line. So we offer up illusions and tricks, the right bait, the right fly, the right lure presented in just the right way at the right time.

Fish cannot, the angler soon finds, be bought or bribed. They do not care "who" we are. They respond best to patience and, finally and primarily, to understanding. For our ancestors, once again, success meant survival. The better they understood the nature of the animals pursued, the better they became at finding and tricking them, and the more successful they were in putting food over the fire.

Today, fishing is a break, a chance to get away from it all. It's a chance for parents and grandparents to connect with children; a chance for adults and children alike to connect with a part of the natural world.

Fishing is part of a lifestyle shared not just with family and friends, but with millions of other anglers, across North America and around the world. The better we know the fish we seek, the better we play this grand game, and knowing these fish better is the purpose of this book. Good angling.

—*Doug Stange*
Editor In Chief, In-Fisherman

Sport Fish of Fresh Water

This is a book that freshwater fishermen in the United States and Canada—from the most seasoned expert to the youngest beginner—have needed for a long time, and now need more than ever.

Of all the continents, North America offers not only the greatest variety of freshwater fishing, but also, and by far, the most opportunities to take advantage of them. Stretching from the frozen Arctic to the sweltering subtropics, and rising from flatlands to snow-topped mountains, North America's geographical diversity assures the presence of a rich and varied aquatic fauna, which include the subjects of this book—an array of nearly 200 species of fish, all of which are important to recreational anglers, most of them because they are either challenging to catch or simply fun to catch. Some species are included, however, because of their immense value as bait or as forage for the popular hook-and-line species.

Not so long ago, it seems, most fishermen had to limit their angling efforts to their own general neighborhoods, rarely traveling farther from home to wet a line than an easy day's round trip by car. Today, however, many modern sportsmen and their sports-minded families are routinely crossing those limits and often traveling great distances to try new and different approaches to an old passion. Today, they might be jigging for Walleye in Lake Erie or Canada; next summer casting for Steelhead in the Pacific Northwest; next winter tossing spinnerbaits at lunker Largemouth Bass in Florida or California.

Not only do anglers now enjoy better and faster means of getting to distant fishing waters than did their grandfathers but also—wonder of wonders—they actually have many more fine fishing destinations to get to.

It's true. Huge expanses of new fishing water have rather recently been created in the form of reservoirs along many major river systems throughout the land. At the same time, access to a wealth of new fishing spots in remote areas of Canada and Alaska have been opened up, and are continuing to open—spots that are perhaps not "new" to natives and a few sportfishing pioneers, but are certainly new to the great numbers of sportsmen who are now able to visit them comfortably and on short schedules.

In addition, sportsmen and fishery managers have been collaborating for much more than a century in programs to supplement natural stocks with hatchery-raised fish, and, in many cases, to introduce new game species to old waters. For instance, Atlantic Striped Bass and Shad have long since been introduced to the Pacific Coast and have established spawning populations. In South Florida, tropical Peacock Bass are stealing some of the thunder from native Largemouths. And in reservoirs from coast to coast, put-and-take fishing for lunker Striped Bass is available to countless inland fishermen who never get a glimpse of the ocean.

Various types of Trout and Salmon have an even more well-traveled background. Brown Trout from Europe are now established in nearly every corner of this continent, while such formerly regional native types as the "western" Rainbow and "eastern" Brook Trout are now to be found at all points of our compass where water quality can support them.

Although most introductions have merely provided a bonus to local angling menus, it's fair to say that stocking programs have played a vital role in pulling Great Lakes fishing from the brink of collapse around the middle of the 20th century, and subsequently helping to transform the Great Lakes into one of the busiest and most productive sportfishing arenas in the world today.

By the mid 1960s, industrial, agricultural and urban pollution around the Lakes had all but ruined the water's ability to support aquatic life and, in addition, a parasitic invader called the Sea Lamprey had destroyed much of the gamefish population that was struggling to survive, especially Lake Trout. To compound those problems, the decline in predatory species had caused an explosion of Alewife and Rainbow Smelt populations. Like the Lamprey, both those baitfishes were alien introductions. Eventually they would become beneficial, but in that perilous period their unfettered growth was causing severe ecological problems throughout the Great Lakes.

Miraculously—or so it seemed to a long-suffering army of Great Lakes anglers—scientists developed an effective chemical control for the Sea Lamprey and introduced their new lampricide in 1958. Eventually it was to kill off some 90 percent of the Lamprey population, and with no harm to other species of fish.

Pollution problems were also being vigorously addressed, finally, by federal, state and regional agencies, and significant improvement was underway.

The important final challenge in the Great Lakes turnaround was that of restoring healthy populations of gamefish while reducing the smothering numbers of forage species. It seemed that both challenges could be met by stocking huge quantities of new predators, specifically Salmons.

But that would not be as easy as it might sound. The Great Lakes already had a long history of introductions, dating back to at least the 1930s. Most of the efforts had been haphazard and unsuccessful—fishery managers merely dumping in quantities of Atlantic Salmon, various Pacific Salmons, three species of Trout and even Arctic Char, and hoping they would "take hold" and begin reproducing huge new populations of their kind. Rainbow and Brown Trout did become established in the Lakes during this period, joining the two native Salmonids, Lake Trout and Brook Trout, but the overall efforts bore little fruit. Even the Rainbows and Browns were pretty much limited to tributary rivers.

With the Lamprey under control and pollution slowly abating, new restocking efforts began in earnest in the sixties. While fishery managers continued to hope that self-sustaining populations of hungry Salmon could be established, they were no longer depending on it. They were preparing to keep pouring in hatchery fish indefinitely, so that—self-sustaining or not—Salmon in the Great Lakes would continue providing quality fishing experiences for millions of anglers for many years to come.

It has been estimated that, since 1966, an average of 61,000 fingerling Salmon have been released into the Great Lakes every day by various fishery agencies of the Lake States and Canada!

So the goal of providing a world-class fishery was achieved but, unfortunately, the goal of controlling Alewives and Smelt was badly overachieved. Management concerns are now directed toward balancing the populations of predators and prey, so that a food base for the Salmon and other predators can be maintained.

Meanwhile, other species of the Great Lakes were also reaping the benefits of improved water quality. In addition to Trout and Salmon, the Lakes are home to such fine gamesters as Smallmouth Bass, Walleye, Perch and Pike, among others. Of those kinds, none is more loved by more fishermen than the Walleye, which is now prospering in the Great Lakes as it never has before within memory, particularly in Lake Erie. Both Walleye and Yellow Perch underwent an explosion in numbers during the 1980s, much to the delight of the many thousands of anglers in that heavily populated part of the world.

Unfortunately, the conquering of the Sea Lamprey did not bring an end to alien invasions in the Great Lakes. Defenses must continue to be maintained against such interlopers as the zebra mussel and Round Goby. And against who-knows-what in the future.

Fishery management in the Great Lakes will always be a monumental undertaking, simply because of the great expanses of water being managed, the array of U.S. and Canadian agencies that are involved in the process and, of course, the huge numbers of citizens that it affects in both countries.

On a much smaller but equally challenging scale, fishery managers in every state and province are also continually striving to keep fish populations steady and water quality high. Their success rate is very high, and getting better every year. Thanks to their efforts and the unprecedented support they now enjoy from the angling public at large, we have never before enjoyed so many quality opportunities to do battle with the Sport Fish of Fresh Water.

How to Use This Book

Many of the freshwater fish that are routinely taken in North America are familiar to anglers in all parts of the United States and over much of Canada. On the other hand, many species are confined to a somewhat limited habitat by temperature, water conditions, or other biological and environmental factors. This means, of course, that anglers who are reasonably familiar with the common sportfish in their usual fishing grounds are pretty sure to encounter an array of new species whenever they travel to another area of the continent—particularly between the Deep South and the far North.

Sill, regardless of whether they work home waters or vacation waters, or whether they chase migratory or resident species, all Atlantic Coast anglers can be sure of one thing: there are so many different kinds of fish out there that anyone who fishes regularly is certain to encounter unfamiliar types from time to time.

In the past, anglers have not had access to a single concise reference to help sort out all the many freshwater species of fish that might end up on the end of a line. The available books have generally fallen into one of two categories—those that cover only a relatively few well-known sport species, or else more scientific volumes that blanket nearly everything with fins, leaving it up to the poor fisherman to dig what he's looking for out of a bewildering assortment of fishes, many of which an angler is never likely to encounter and many more that are of no interest at all to the sportsman.

This book is designed strictly for the recreational fisherman and is aimed at describing and illustrating virtually every species an angler is ever likely to find on the end of his line or in his bait bucket anywhere in the United States and Canada—from the Arctic to the subtropics, from the Atlantic Ocean to the Gulf of Mexico to the Pacific. Even far out in the Pacific to the westernmost state, Hawaii.

Yes, all the potential hook-and-line catches are here—nearly 200 of them—panfish, prestigious gamefish and irritating pests alike. The most popular and productive baitfish are included, as are many of those "insignificant" little types which mean nothing to adult anglers but, since

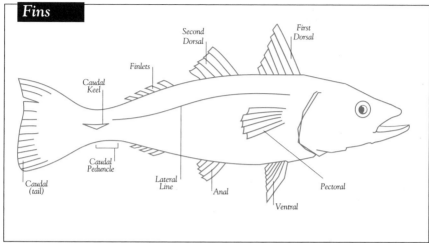

Fins

Second Dorsal

First Dorsal

Finlets

Caudal Keel

Caudal Peduncle

Caudal (tail)

Lateral Line

Anal

Ventral

Pectoral

Here's a typical configuration of fins useful for identification.

they provide an exciting introduction to fishing for so many youngsters, also deserve the name of sportfish.

More than just a guide to identification, the book provides essential basic information concerning where and how to go after them, and how each species rates in fighting ability and table quality.

It would be nice if all the fish in the book could be sorted into neat chapters according to region. Then the local angler could find all his potential catches in one section. Sadly, though, such a neat arrangement is impossible, because the majority of covered species are at home in a variety of water depths and environments, over many different regions.

For lack of any more logical arrangement, most chapters in the book cover a single family of fishes. This makes for handy identification because related types almost always share certain common characteristics. In a few cases, however, species from two or more families are included in the same chapter because they share similar characteristics, or simply because they are individuals and share space with other individuals.

THE INDIVIDUAL ENTRIES

For ease of reference, the entry for every fish in the book is broken down into categories that answer the most common questions asked by fishermen about their catch. Each entry is headed by the most widely used common name, along with the scientific name and, of course, the color illustration. Because common names are anything but consistent, the scientific name is the only truly correct label. Other information is given as follows:

DESCRIPTION: Since individuals of any species can vary from the typical coloration and markings, it is important to consult both the illustration and the written description to assure positive identification.

OTHER NAMES: These are some of the more popular common names heard for the species—but probably not the only ones used in one region or another.

RANGE: Outlines the range, in Canada and the United States only, where the described species is commonly found. Note that many fish have far wider ranges, which may cover several countries or continents, especially since so many kinds of fish are now being transplanted to new waters—both deliberately and accidentally.

WHERE TO FISH: Tells the preferred hangouts of adult fish, but it should go without saying that most species of sportfish roam widely and are often caught in nontypical settings.

SIZE: Describes the usual size range of specimens taken by sportsmen. In most cases, estimates of the potential maximum size are also included.

FOOD VALUE: The table quality of a particular fish is highly subjective. The information here is based on established culinary reputation and on the author's personal opinion.

GAME QUALITIES: Again, this is based on the author's long personal experience and on extensive consultation with other anglers.

TACKLE: Recommends the most suitable types of tackle for both efficiency and good sport.

BAITS AND LURES: Notes a few standard or especially effective baits and lures. Experienced anglers will realize, however, that there is plenty of room for other choices.

PREFERRED TEMPERATURE RANGES
Popular Freshwater Species

All kinds of fish are more active when the water temperature falls within a certain range. With luck, that activity will include eager feeding. Best comfort zones for many of our favorite hook-and-line fishes are noted below in Fahrenheit degrees, but one must remember that in every case it is possible to catch fish both above and below the stated range. Which takes us back to the best angling advice of all—go fishing whenever you can.

These tables will be most helpful in large lakes and streams, where varying depth and current can cause a great variation in water temperature.

	SPECIES	TEMPERATURE RANGE
BLACK BASSES	Largemouth	80-82
	Smallmouth	65-73
	Spotted	70-78
	Rock	62-72
STRIPED BASSES	Striper	65-70
	White	66-75
	Whiterock	70-80
	White Perch	75-85
SUNFISHES	Bluegill	69-85
	Green	75-87
	Longear	70-80
	Pumpkinseed	71-82
	Redbreast	70-80
	Black Crappie	70-75
	White Crappie	61-71

continued

SPECIES		TEMPERATURE RANGE
PIKES	Muskellunge	63-78
	Northern Pike	55-65
	Chain Pickerel	66-80
	Grass Pickerel	66-80
WALLEYE & PERCH	Walleye	59-68
	Sauger	66-70
	Yellow Perch	66-77
CATFISHES	Channel	70-87
	Blue	70-80
	Flathead	82-88
	White	70-88
	Bullheads	70-83
SALMONS	Atlantic	50-62
	Landlocked	45-58
	Chinook	50-63
	Chum	48-57
	Coho	44-57
	Kokanee	50-57
	Pink	49-57
	Sockeye	50-59
TROUTS	Brook	45-61
	Brown	56-65
	Cutthroat	50-65
	Golden	50-60
	Lake	40-55
	Rainbow	50-70
	Steelhead	48-52

	SPECIES	TEMPERATURE RANGE
STURGEONS	Atlantic	66-70
	White	63-65
OTHERS	Arctic Char	53-61
	Grayling	47-52
	Mt. Whitefish	48-52
	Cisco	52-55
	Bowfin	65-80
	Buffalo	81-90
	Carp	79-84
	Drum	68-76
	Goldeye	70-77
	Mooneye	72-81
	Shad, Common	59-70
	Gars	80-92
	Suckers	60-80

FISH FOR THE TABLE

Although catch-and-release is standard practice today among sport anglers, that doesn't mean they must give up the enjoyment of regular fish dinners. Even the heavily pressured species—Bass and Trout, for example—can be eaten without a guilty conscience when they are brought home in compliance with the strict regulations that now prevail in all jurisdictions.

One common and very effective management tool is the slot limit, which allows anglers to take a small bag of fish that are large enough to have spawned at least once, yet still below the size that makes up the most important segment of the breeding population. Another effective modern approach to protecting pressured stocks has been simply to establish different bag limits for different waters rather than apply the same rules throughout an entire state or jurisdiction. This allows certain lakes or streams to be designated, say, as catch-and-release waters and managed for quality fish, while other waterways are managed (or stocked) to produce big numbers of smaller fish, allowing reasonable harvest by anglers.

Happier still for all who love fish on the table is the fact that many of our most delicious freshwater species are prolific breeders that can easily withstand substantial harvesting and, consequently, carry quite liberal catch allowances. These include, but are by no means limited to, Perch, Crappie, Bluegill, and White and Yellow Bass, as well as Bullheads and other kinds of Catfish.

Fish ranks among the healthiest of foods. Certain oily fleshed kinds of fish, particularly Salmon, contain Omega-3 fatty acids, which help provide protection against heart disease and some other major health threats. While the majority of freshwater fish have lean flesh and lack those essential fatty acids, they still contain other important nutrients and are low in saturated fat. Heart-conscious anglers can even enjoy fried fish, provided they cook them in olive or canola oil—monounsaturated oils that are not merely permissible but actually beneficial in holding down cholesterol.

On the other side of the fish-eating coin we have the all-too-common warnings these days against eating certain fish—or rather, eating too many meals of certain species taken from certain waters. Great Lakes Salmon fall into this unhappy category because of residual pollutants; however, similar warnings exist for Largemouth Bass and other predatory species from coast to coast. Many of the warnings are due to high levels of mercury in the flesh, a contaminant that appears to occur naturally in many waters and does not necessarily involve man-made pollutants.

Health warnings, whatever the cause or reason, generally advise eating the subject species only in limited amounts and at certain intervals. Pregnant women and persons with particular health problems may be advised to eat none at all, in some cases.

Anglers should keep abreast of advisories for their own territory. That sort of information is widely disseminated. It can be obtained from fishery management agencies, newspapers, bait and tackle shops and numerous other sources.

FISHERY MANAGEMENT AND LAWS

Happily, many sportsmen these days are not only abiding by size and bag limits, but also are going the extra mile by releasing most of their fish, whether legally required or not. This practice, obviously, is of great importance in helping to maintain good populations of many game species that have been undergoing ever-increasing pressure from anglers and, in certain cases, from commercial overfishing as well.

Rigid fishery management practices have been put in place by every state and province—and also by the U.S. and Canadian governments in cases where federal areas are involved, or where anadromous species, such as Salmon and Striped Bass are concerned. As a result, some previously troubled species are discernibly on the upswing, while the steady depletion of others has been slowed drastically, if not yet eliminated.

All this has led to a sometimes highly confusing assortment of laws, compounded by the fact that these laws—permitting and catch limits in particular—often vary a great deal from state to state, province to province, or even from water to water within a single jurisdiction. Because so many jurisdictions are involved, and because the rules are constantly being revised, even a general outline of the many rules and laws is impossible to give in any one book. Suffice it to say that an important part of any angler's homework these days is to be fully aware of the laws and to carefully observe all legal requirements.

Every angler must be sure to check and abide by all licensing requirements and fishing laws. Information is available at most tackle and bait shops, or directly from the various state and provincial agencies, listed here:

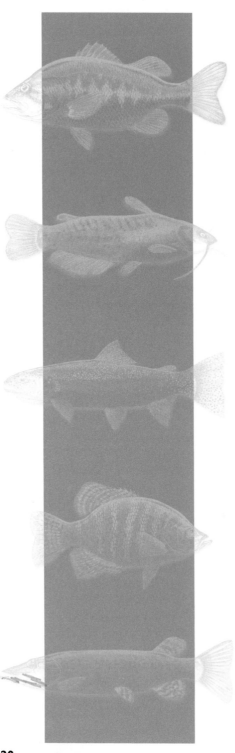

STATE AND PROVINCIAL FISHERY AGENCIES
U.S. and CANADA

UNITED STATES

Alabama Division of Wildlife and Freshwater Fisheries
64 N. Union St.
Montgomery, AL 36130-3020
(334) 242-3471
www.dcnr.state.al.us/agfd

Alaska Dept. of Fish and Game
P.O. Box 25526
Juneau, AK 99802-5526
(907) 465-4180
www.state.ak.us/adfg

Arizona Game & Fish Dept.
2222 W. Greenway Rd.
Phoenix, AZ 85023-4399
(602) 942-3000
www.azgfd.us

Arkansas Game and Fish Commission
2 Natural Resources Dr.
Little Rock, AR 72205
(501) 223-6371
www.agfc.com

Dept. of Fish and Game
Fisheries Program Branch
1416 9th St.
Sacramento, CA 95814
(916) 653-7664
www.dfg.ca.gov

Colorado Division of Wildlife
6060 Broadway
Denver, CO 80216
(303) 297-1192
www.wildlife.state.co.us

Connecticut Dept. of Environmental Protection
79 Elm St.
Hartford, CT 06106-5127
(860) 424-3474
www.dep.state.ct.us

Delaware Division of Fish and Wildlife
89 Kings Hwy.
Dover, DE 19901
(302) 739-3441
www.fw.delaware.gov

Florida Fish and Wildlife Conservation Commission
620 South Meridian St.
Tallahassee, FL 32399-1600
(850) 488-0331
www.floridaconservation.org

Georgia Wildlife Resources Division
2070 U.S. Hwy. 278, S.E.
Social Circle, GA 30279
(770) 918-6418
www.georgiawildlife.dnr.state.ga.us

**Hawaii Division
of Aquatic Resources**
1151 Punchbowl St.
Room 330
Honolulu, HI 96813
(808) 587-0100
www.state.hi.us/dlnr/dar

Idaho Fish and Game
P.O. Box 25
Boise, ID 83707
(208) 334-3700
www.fishandgame.idaho.gov

Illinois Division of Fisheries
1 Natural way
Springfield, IL 62702
(217) 782-6424
www.dnr.state.il.us/fish

**Indiana Division
of Fish and Wildlife**
402 W. Washington St., W273
Indianapolis, IN 46204
(317) 232-4080
www.state.in.us/dnr/fishwild

Iowa DNR Fisheries Bureau
502 E. 9th St.
Wallace State Office Building
Des Moines, IA 50319-0034
(515) 281-3474
www.iowadnr.com/fish/index.html

**Kansas Dept. of Wildlife
and Parks**
900 SW Jackson St., Suite 502
Topeka, KS 66612-1233
(785) 296-2281
www.kdwp.state.ks.us/fishing/fishing.html

**Kentucky Dept. of Fish and
Wildlife Resources**
#1 Game Farm Rd.
Frankfort, KY 40601
(800) 858-1549
www.kdfwr.state.ky.us

**Louisiana Inland
Fisheries Division**
2000 Quail Dr.
Baton Rouge, LA 70808
(225) 765-2330
www.wlf.state.la.us

**Maine Dept. of Inland
Fisheries and Wildlife**
284 State St.
41 State House Station
Augusta, ME 04333-0041
(207) 287-8000
www.state.me.us/ifw

**Maryland DNR
Fisheries Service**
Tawes Building, B-2
Taylor Ave.
Annapolis, MD 21401
(410) 260-8281
www.dnr.state.md.us/fisheries

**Massachusetts Division
of Fisheries & Wildlife**
251 Causeway St., Suite 400
Boston, MA 02114-2152
(617) 626-1590
www.state.ma.us/dfwele/dfw

Michigan Dept.
of Natural Resources
Fisheries Division
P.O. Box 30446
Lansing, MI 48909
(517) 373-1280
www.dnr.state.mi.us

Minnesota Dept.
of Natural Resources
500 Lafayette Rd.
St. Paul, MN 55155-4040
(651) 296-6157
www.dnr.state.mn.us

Mississippi Dept. of Wildlife,
Fisheries and Parks
1505 Eastover Dr.
Jackson, MS 39211-6374
(601) 432-2400
www.mdwfp.com

Missouri Dept.
of Conservation
P.O. Box 180
Jefferson City, MO 65102
(573) 751-4115
www.mdc.mo.gov/fish

Montana Fish,
Wildlife and Parks
P.O. Box 8009
Helena, MT 59604-8009
(406) 444-2535
www.fwp.state.mt.us

Nebraska Game
and Parks Commission
2200 North 33rd St.
Lincoln, NE 68503
(402) 471-0641
www.ngpc.state.ne.us

Nevada Division of Wildlife
P.O. Box 10678
Reno, NV 89520-0022
(775) 688-1500
www.nevadadivisionofwildlife.org

New Hampshire Fish
and Game Dept.
2 Hazen Dr.
Concord, NH 03301
(603) 271-3211
www.wildlife.state.nh.us

New Jersey Division
of Fish and Wildlife
P.O. Box 400
Trenton NJ 08625-0400
(609) 292-1599
www.state.nj.us/dep/fgw

New Mexico Dept.
of Game and Fish
P.O. Box 25112
Santa Fe, NM 87504
(800) 862-9310
www.wildlife.state.nm.us

New York State Division of Fish, Wildlife and Marine Resources
625 Broadway
Albany, NY 12233-4790
(518) 402-8920
www.dec.ny.gov

North Carolina Wildlife Resources Commission
1721 Mail Service Center
Raleigh, NC 27699-1721
(919) 733-3633
www.wildlife.state.nc.us

North Dakota Game and Fish Dept.
100 N. Bismarck Exp.
Bismarck, ND 58501-5095
(701) 328-6300
www.gf.nd.gov

Ohio Division of Wildlife
1840 Belcher Dr.
Columbus, OH 43224-1329
(614) 265-6300
www.dnr.state.oh.us/wildlife

Oklahoma Dept. of Wildlife Conservation
1801 N. Lincoln —
Oklahoma City, OK 73105
(405) 521-3851
www.wildlifedepartment.com

Oregon Dept. of Fish and Wildlife
P.O. Box 59
Portland, OR 97207
(503) 872-5252
www.dfw.state.or.us

Pennsylvania Fish and Boat Commission
P.O. Box 67000
Harrisburg, PA 17106-7000
(814) 359-5154
www.fish.state.pa.us

Rhode Island Division of Fish and Wildlife
4808 Tower Hill Rd.
Wakefield, RI 02879
(401) 789-3094
www.state.ri.us/dem/programs/bnatres/fishwild/index.htm

South Carolina Dept. of Natural Resources
1000 Assembly St.
Columbia, SC 29201
(803) 734-3888
www.dnr.sc.gov/fish.html

South Dakota Dept. of Game, Fish and Parks
523 East Capital Ave.
Pierre, SD 57501-3182
(605) 773-3485
www.state.sd.us/gfp

Tennessee Wildlife

Resources Agency
Ellington Agricultural Center
P.O. Box 40747
Nashville, TN 37204
(615) 781-6575
www.state.tn.us/twra

Texas Parks and Wildlife
4200 Smith School Rd.
Austin, TX 78744
(512) 389-4800
www.tpwd.state.tx.us

**Utah Division of
Wildlife Resources**
P.O. Box 146301
Salt Lake City, UT 84114-6301
(801) 538-4700
www.wildlife.utah.gov

**Vermont Fish and
Wildlife Dept.**
10 South
103 South Main St.
Waterbury, VT 05671-0501
(802) 241-3700
www.anr.state.vt.us/fw/fwhome

**Virginia Dept. of Game
and Inland Fisheries**
4010 West Broad St.
Richmond VA 23230
(804) 367-1000
www.dgif.state.va.us

Washington Dept.

of Fish and Wildlife
600 Capitol Way North
Olympia, WA 98501-1091
(360) 902-2700
www.wdfw.wa.gov

**West Virginia Division
of Natural Resources**
Wildlife Resources Section
State Capitol Building 3
Room 812
Charleston, WV 25305
(304) 558-2771
www.dnr.state.wv.us/wvfishing

**Wisconsin Fisheries
Management & Habitat
Protection**
P.O. Box 7921
101 S. Webster St.
Madison, WI 53707
(608) 267-7498
www.dnr.wi.gov

**Wyoming Game and Fish
Dept.**
5400 Bishop Blvd.
Cheyenne, WY 82006
(307) 777-4600
www.gf.state.wy.us

Alberta Fisheries and Wildlife Management Division
Main Floor, South Tower,
Petroleum Plaza
9915 0 108 St., Edmonton, Alberta
T5K 2G8
(780) 944-0313
http://www3.gov.ab.ca/srd/fw/fishing

Manitoba Fisheries
200 Saulteaux Crescent
Winnipeg, Manitoba
MB R3J 3W3
(204) 945-6640

New Brunswick Dept. of Natural Resources
P.O. Box 6000
Fredericton, N.B.
E3B 5H1
(506) 453-3826
http://www.gov.nb.ca/0078/fw/index_fw.asp

Newfoundland and Labrador Forest Resources
P.O. Box 8700
St. John's, Newfoundland
A1B 4J6
(709) 729-4715

Northwest Territories Wildlife and Fisheries
600, 5102-50th Ave.
Yellowknife, NT
X1A 3S8
(867) 920 8064
http://www.nwtwildlife.rwed.gov.nt.ca

Nova Scotia Department of Natural Resources, Wildlife Division
http://www.gov.ns.ca/NATR/wildlife/index.htm

Ontario Ministry of Natural Resources
P.O. Box 7000
Peterborough, Ontario
K9J 8M5
(800) 667-1940
http://www.mnr.gov.on.ca/MNR/fwmenu.html

Prince Edward Island Fisheries
P.O. Box 2000
Charlottetown, PE
C1A 7N8
(902) 368-5000
http://www.gov.pe.ca/ft/index.php3

**Quebec Ministry
of Wildlife and Parks**
675, boulevard RenÈ-LÈvesque
Est, boÓte 93
QuÈbec (QuÈbec)
GIR 5V7
(418) 521-3845
*http://www.fapaq.gouv.qc.ca/en/
index1.htm*

**Saskatchewan Environment
and Resource Management**
Room 140, 3211 Albert St.
Regina, SK
S4S 5W6
(306) 787-2700
http://www.serm.gov.sk.ca/fishwild

**Yukon Dept. of
Renewable Resources**
10 Burns Rd.
Whitehorse, Yukon
YIA 4Y9
(867) 667-5652
http://www.renres.gov.yk.ca

By all odds, the Largemouth Bass is the No. 1 favorite among American fishermen. The reasons are almost too numerous to list, but the main ones are its widespread availability and its willingness—often eagerness—to pounce on a variety of baits and lures. Although a warm-water species, it is adaptable to a reasonably broad range of temperatures and so is found in at least some waters of every state except Alaska, and also in southern Canada. There are several races of Largemouth, the largest being the Florida subspecies, which has been introduced into other states to increase size. The result? Lunker "Florida" Bass now being caught in Texas and California are often larger than Florida's leading catches. California harbors the biggest Bass of all, having recorded several catches of 20 pounds or more. One California fish even came within a few ounces of the record 22-pound, 4-ounce catch made 70 years ago in Georgia. The Smallmouth Bass is a stronger fighter, pound-for-pound, than the Largemouth, and also better on the table. It prefers cooler environs than the Largemouth and in some waters co-exists happily with cold-water Trout. While common in many cool lakes, the Smallmouth seems to prefer living in streams. The same can be said for the Spotted Bass, Redeye Bass, Shoal Bass, Suwannee Bass and Guadelupe Bass, the other members of this popular group. As for size, the Smallmouth sometimes exceeds 10 pounds, and the Spotted Bass may come close to that figure. The Shoal is next largest and specimens of 7 or 8 pounds are on record. The other three species rarely exceed 2 pounds.

The Black Basses

Largemouth Bass

Smallmouth Bass

Spotted Bass

Suwannee Bass

Guadelupe Bass

Redeye Bass

Shoal Bass

Largemouth Bass

Micropterus salmoides

OTHER NAMES:

Black Bass
Green Bass
Bigmouth Bass
Oswego Bass
Green Trout

RANGE: *Native to the eastern half of the United States and northeastern Mexico, it is now well established in all states except Alaska, as well as waters in southern Canada.*

WHERE TO FISH: *Largemouth inhabit all kinds of warm water but are most plentiful in ponds, lakes and slow rivers where there is plenty of vegetation. Best fishing generally is close to cover or inside it, although they do school in open water at times, chasing baitfish.*

DESCRIPTION: Dominant color is green, ranging from light to almost black, depending mostly on water where caught. Usually has a longitudinal patchy stripe from eye to tail. Front and rear portions of dorsal fin are separated. Maxillary (jaw) extends rearward to point beyond the eye.

SIZE: Catches everywhere average 1-3 pounds, but individuals up to 6 pounds or so are taken with fair frequency throughout its range. The maximum in northern areas is about 10 pounds or slightly more. In California, Texas, Florida and the Deep South, occasional fish run to more than 15 pounds and rare ones to around 20. World record 22 pounds, 4 ounces.

FOOD VALUE: Varies greatly according to size of the fish and specific habitat. Small "keepers," or fish that meet size or slot limits, are usually very good if skinned.

GAME QUALITIES: Aggressive nature, acrobatic ability and fair strength make it a challenge on any light gear.

TACKLE: In fairly open water any size line is adequate, but heavy tests are required when fishing thick weeds or snag-filled reservoirs. Baitcasting and spinning lead in popularity, but the Largemouth is also a great fish for the fly rod.

LURES AND BAITS: There seems to be no limit to the Bigmouth's appetite, whether for natural prey or artificial. Among the former, shiners and other small fish lead the angler's arsenal, with salamanders, frogs and crayfish joining in at times. By far the most productive artificials are plastic worms, eels and salamanders. Spinnerbaits, jigs, weedless spoons, topwater plugs and crankbaits figure prominently as well. Fly fishermen favor popping bugs and large, undulating streamers but, as with hard lures, many designs may draw strikes from Bass of all sizes.

Smallmouth Bass

Micropterus dolomieu

DESCRIPTION: Bronze or brownish above, with brown-green sides and dark bars. Underparts are yellowish. Dorsal fin is continuous but has a shallow notch. The upper jaw projects to a point under the eye—not past it.

SIZE: Most run 1-2 pounds. Smallmouth of 4 pounds and heavier are prizes, but not too unusual in many places. Maximum is about 10 pounds or slightly more. World record 10 pounds, 14 ounces.

FOOD VALUE: Excellent.

GAME QUALITIES: Very strong, fast, active and a good jumper, the Smallmouth owns a well-deserved reputation as the best fighter of the Black Bass group.

TACKLE: Snags are seldom a problem in Smallmouth fishing and so light spinning and baitcasting gear will give the best sport. Fly tackle also produces well in many situations.

LURES AND BAITS: The leading Smallmouth lures probably are jigs, especially when bounced along bottom in imitation of crawfish. Crankbaits and spinners also do consistently good work in nearly all situations, while surface lures produce when the fishing scene is fairly shallow. Crawfish, hellgrammites, nightcrawlers and small fish are among the top natural baits.

OTHER NAMES:

Black Bass
Brown Bass
Bronzeback

RANGE: *Originally from southern Quebec and the Great Lakes to about the mid-South. Now has a broad range across southern Canada, and is found in some waters of all states except Alaska, Florida and Louisiana. Needs cooler maximum temperatures than the Largemouth Bass.*

WHERE TO FISH: *Smallmouth love fairly fast-flowing streams, but are also at home in rock-strewn lakes. Rocky areas hold the key to angling success in any kind of Smallmouth water. In lakes where Smallmouth and Largemouth co-exist, Smallmouth are more likely to be found in cooler, rocky sectors, while Largemouth favor warmer, vegetated areas.*

Spotted Bass

Micropterus punctulatus

OTHER NAMES:

Kentucky Bass
Spot

RANGE: *From southern Indiana, Ohio and West Virginia to the Gulf of Mexico and west to eastern Texas. The South Atlantic states have spotted bass only in their westernmost regions.*

WHERE TO FISH: *This fish is found mostly in clear streams and in cool reservoirs and lakes. Stream fish prefer the deeper pools. In reservoirs, the Spotted Bass is caught at greater depths than other kinds of Bass—sometimes 100 feet or more.*

DESCRIPTION: Green above; yellow to white below. There is a dark stripe the full length of the side, usually in the form of connected patches. Numerous small spots on lower side. Dark spot at base of tail grows lighter with age. Shallow notch in dorsal fin. Upper jaw extends about as far as the rear edge of the eye.

SIZE: One pound is a good average, and a 3-pounder is a prize. Fish over 5 pounds are rare, but the potential is to 8 or 9 pounds in large lakes. World record 10 pounds, 4 ounces.

FOOD VALUE: Excellent.

GAME QUALITIES: For its size, a terrific battler, whether hooked shallow or deep. Good jumper, too.

TACKLE: Spinning and baitcasting tackle with light lines. Fly fishing gets fish too, especially in streams.

LURES AND BAITS: Very much the same as for Smallmouth Bass. Jigs shine for deep fishing. In rivers and shallows, spinnerbaits and small crankbaits are good, along with worms and other plastics and, at times, topwater plugs. Crawfish, hellgrammites, salamanders and worms head a long list of productive natural baits.

Guadelupe Bass

Micropterus treculi

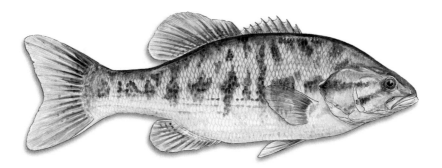

DESCRIPTION: Similar to the Spotted Bass, but the bands on the sides are larger and darker. The upper jaw does not extend past the eye, and the eye is red.

SIZE: Usually less than 12 inches; occasionally tops 2 pounds. World record 3 pounds, 11 ounces.

FOOD VALUE: Very good.

GAME QUALITIES: A scrappy foe for its size.

TACKLE: Performs best on ultralight spinning gear and light fly outfits.

LURES AND BAITS: Small crankbaits. Spinnerbaits, jigs and artificial worms. For natural bait try crawfish, minnows or nightcrawlers.

RANGE: The Guadeloupe, Colorado and San Antonio river systems in Central Texas.

WHERE TO FISH: Deep pools and eddies in streams; rocky areas in lakes.

Suwannee Bass

Micropterus notius

RANGE: *Found only in North Florida and extreme South Georgia, mostly in the Suwannee River and its tributaries, but also, and to a lesser extent, in the Ochlockonee River system a bit farther west.*

WHERE TO FISH: *Except in times of high water, Suwannee Bass prefer the middle reaches of the stream to the edges. It likes swifter water than the Largemouth Bass, and often hangs around in deep, rock-strewn pools.*

DESCRIPTION: Background color is tan or deep gold with numerous dark brown markings. Belly is silvery, tinged with blue. The eye is red.

SIZE: Most catches weigh less than a pound, and a 2-pounder is a giant. World record 3 pounds, 14 ounces.

FOOD VALUE: Excellent.

GAME QUALITIES: Possibly even more aggressive than the Largemouth and, pound for pound, a stronger fighter.

TACKLE: Light spinning, baitcasting and fly.

LURES AND BAITS: Thin balsa plugs are excellent, as are a variety of small crankbaits. Spinnerbaits, in-line spinners and artificial worms are other favorites. Top naturals include crawfish, small minnows and earthworms.

Redeye Bass

Micropterus coosae

DESCRIPTION: Green or olive above, white below, with dark bars on sides. Tail is red or orange and the eye is red.

SIZE: Rarely over 2 pounds.

FOOD VALUE: Very good.

GAME QUALITIES: Difficult to fool, but a hard fighter and good jumper once hooked.

TACKLE: Light spinning, fly and baitcasting.

LURES AND BAITS: In-line spinners, small plastic worms and small surface plugs rank among the best hard lures. Fly fishermen do well with popping bugs and large wet flies and nymphs. Insects make up a prominent part of the diet, but worms, crawfish and minnows are the most-used natural baits.

OTHER NAMES:

Coosa Bass

RANGE: *Mobile basin in Alabama, Coosa and Tallapoosa drainages into western South Carolina. Introduced into Tennessee and Kentucky.*

WHERE TO FISH: *This Bass prefers clear, running water with rocky bottom, or large pools in small creeks.*

Shoal Bass

Micropterus cataractae

DESCRIPTION: Long confused with the Redeye Bass, the Shoal Bass was considered the same species (although a different race) before being reclassified in 1999. This fish is a darker green than the Redeye Bass and the stripes are usually more vivid. There is a dark blotch and three black lines on the gill cover. The eye is red. An obvious distinguishing feature is the tail fin, which is dark green or black, not red.

SIZE: Averages 1-3 pounds. Reaches 7 or 8 pounds on rare occasion. World record 8 pounds, 12 ounces.

FOOD VALUE: Very good.

GAME QUALITIES: Not easy to fool and a very tough fighter for its size.

TACKLE: Light spinning, baitcasting and fly tackle.

LURES AND BAITS: Small spinners and small plastic worms work well, as do small crankbaits and surface plugs. Best naturals are crawfish, minnows and worms.

OTHER NAMES:

Redeye Bass

Flint River Smallmouth

RANGE: *The Flint and Chattahoochee River systems of Georgia and Alabama and the Apalachicola and Chipola systems of Florida.*

WHERE TO FISH: *Rocky shoal areas, particularly pools below rapids.*

M ost of the fish that the nation refers to as "panfish" are Sunfishes and belong to the same family as the Black Basses. So do the little Rock Basses. The Sunfishes will be covered in the next chapter, but the Rock Basses are here being dealt with separately because, unlike the Sunnies, their appearance and aggressiveness seem to mark them as miniature copies of their larger and more highly publicized kin. Their appetites are similar too. These little fellows happily hit nearly every variety of Bass lure, including many full-size models. The three rarer species live in cool, flowing water and are seldom found in a lake or pond—at least in one that isn't fed by substantial streams. Devoted seekers of Smallmouth Bass tend to look upon the Rock Basses as pests, but those who deliberately pursue the little fellows usually find good sport, tasty eating and a target that isn't too difficult to fool. And, despite their lack of heft, they provide a fair amount of excitement on ultralight spinning gear or light fly tackle. The common Rock Bass is widely distributed, whereas others in this group are limited to particular geographic areas, where, in some streams, they co-exist with the common Rock Bass and may not be distinguished by most fishermen.

The Rock Basses

Ozark Bass

Roanoke Bass

Rock Bass

Shadow Bass

Ozark Bass

Ambloplites constellatus

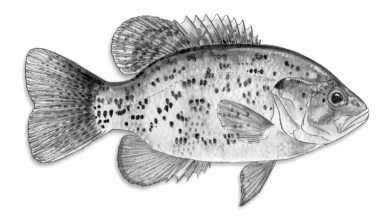

OTHER NAMES:

Rock Bass

RANGE: *Native only to the White River and its tributaries in Arkansas and Missouri, but introduced to a few other waters.*

WHERE TO FISH: *Likes rocky pools of streams, but also hangs around shoreline rocks, logs and vegetation.*

DESCRIPTION: Color is much like that of the Rock Bass and other close kin, but the Ozark Bass is distinguishable by the numerous small black dots scattered over its side.

SIZE: Less than one-half pound. World record 1 pound.

FOOD VALUE: Very good.

GAME QUALITIES: Tough but a lightweight.

TACKLE: Pole, fly, ultralight spinning.

LURES AND BAITS: Minnows, worms and insect baits. Nymphs and popping bugs are productive as are very small hard lures.

Roanoke Bass

Ambloplites cavifrons

DESCRIPTION: Lighter in overall color than the Rock Bass, this fish is greenish or tan above. Both light and dark side blotches. Small white or yellow dots mark the upper sides and head.

SIZE: Averages a half-pound or less; rarely tops 1 pound. World record 1 pound, 5 ounces.

FOOD VALUE: Very good.

GAME QUALITIES: Good fight for a little fellow.

TACKLE: Pole, ultralight spinning, fly.

LURES AND BAITS: Most are caught on worms, minnows and insect baits. Will also take flies and small lures.

OTHER NAMES:

Rock Bass
Perch

RANGE: *Found in only a few streams in the central border areas of Virginia and North Carolina.*

WHERE TO FISH: *Pools of clear, flowing streams. Likes sand or rock bottom.*

Rock Bass

Ambloplites rupestris

OTHER NAMES:

Goggle-eye
Black Perch
Rock Sunfish
Redeye

RANGE: *Border areas from Quebec to Saskatchewan in Canada, then south to northern Georgia and Alabama. Widely introduced elsewhere.*

WHERE TO FISH: *Rock Bass are common in many Smallmouth Bass waters; perhaps most numerous in flowing streams, where they hold in pools or over rocky bottom. Also around rocky or bushy banks of both lakes and streams.*

DESCRIPTION: This and the other three species are often confused with and all are often called Rock Bass, but this one is by far the largest and most prominent. It is a chunky fish with green back, dark blotches on the side, and rows of small black dots below the lateral line.

SIZE: Averages well under a pound, but occasionally tops 2 pounds. World record 3 pounds.

FOOD VALUE: A tasty panfish.

GAME QUALITIES: Very pugnacious and often hits large lures. Strikes hard and resists as well as its small size allows.

TACKLE: Pole, ultralight spinning, fly.

LURES AND BAITS: Takes almost anything in the way of popular natural baits, but mostly minnows, worms and cut baits. An excellent fly fish, especially on popping bugs and small streamers. Best hard lures are little jigs and spinners.

Shadow Bass

Ambloplites ariommus

DESCRIPTION: Overall color is brownish, with large and slightly darker "shadows" or blotches marking the sides. The eye is red and very large.

SIZE: Seldom tops half a pound; most are smaller. World record 1 pound, 13 ounces.

FOOD VALUE: Tasty panfish.

GAME QUALITIES: Tough but a lightweight.

TACKLE: Pole, ultralight spinning.

LURES AND BAITS: Worms, crickets, minnows, very tiny in-line spinners and jigs.

OTHER NAMES:

Rock Bass

RANGE: *From western Georgia and the Florida Panhandle to Louisiana, Arkansas and southern Missouri.*

WHERE TO FISH: *Small, clear streams.*

Although Black Bass anglers might argue, it's likely that more fishermen go after Sunfishes of various kinds than any other angling targets in fresh water. The familiar image of the freckle-faced youngster fishing with a makeshift pole is an accurate one but far from typical. Anglers of every age and economic status use every sort of light tackle to pursue the many members of the Sunfish group, which may get its collective name from the generally round shape of most members, or from the colorful reds and yellows with which many of them are adorned. In the South, these fish are collectively called Bream, rather than Sunfish. Regardless, all are highly adaptable to various temperatures and water conditions, and this makes them easy to establish in areas where they are not native. It's safe to say that all the lower states and most Canadian provinces are home to various kinds of Sunfishes. Each species of course, has its own name too—usually, in fact, two or more different names that vary by region. Possibly the Bluegill and the two species of Crappie are the best-known and most-caught varieties. Others that rank near the top are the Pumpkinseed and Redbreast. Numerous kinds of midget Sunfishes are also found in our waters but aren't treated here because they are too small to hold much appeal for fishermen.

The Sunfishes

Sacramento Perch

Black Crappie

White Crappie

Flier

Warmouth

Bluegill

Pumpkinseed

Redear Sunfish

Redbreast Sunfish

Spotted Sunfish

Longear Sunfish

Green Sunfish

Sacramento Perch

Archoplites interruptus

RANGE: The only native Sunfish west of the Rockies, its natural range includes the Sacramento-San Joaquin river system, the Pajaro and Salinas Rivers, and Clear Lake, all in California. It is now uncommon, however, except in various stocked ponds and lakes of California, Nevada and Utah.

WHERE TO FISH: Best lake fishing takes place in spawning season over hard bottom; at other times the larger fish forage over plant beds.

DESCRIPTION: Brown back with white or gray sides, heavily mottled. There are several dark vertical bars on the side and a horizontal line across the gill cover.

SIZE: It frequently tops one pound and often exceeds 2 pounds. World record 3 pounds, 3 ounces.

FOOD VALUE: Very good.

GAME QUALITIES: The fight is strong and bass-like.

TACKLE: Spinning and baitcasting. Fly fishing is seldom as productive.

LURES AND BAITS: Unlike most panfish it seldom takes worms, preferring small baitfish. Spinners are the artificials chosen by most anglers.

Black Crappie

Pomoxis nigromaculatus

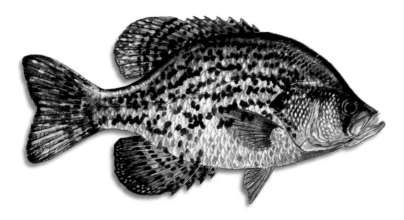

DESCRIPTION: Green or dark gray on back, shading to white or yellow on the sides. Sides are marked with many spots and wavy, broken lines. The tail and rear dorsal fins are large and fan-like.

SIZE: Most catches run 8-12 ounces, but fish weighing 1-2 pounds are pretty common. Potential maximum is more than 4 pounds. World record 4 pounds, 8 ounces.

FOOD VALUE: Excellent.

GAME QUALITIES: Fair. Less active on a line than most other panfish of similar size.

TACKLE: Poles top the list, but ultralight spinning gear also takes many Crappie. Fly tackle can sometimes be successful for the determined angler, but is not consistently productive.

LURES AND BAITS: Nothing beats a live minnow, but dead minnows and cut strips of fish are pretty good. Worms, shrimp and insects will work, too. Tiny jigs lead the artificial pack, but small spinners are productive too, and small crankbaits will take some of the biggest specimens.

OTHER NAMES:

Speckled Perch
Speck
Calico Bass
Papermouth
Strawberry Bass

RANGE: Easily transplanted, the Black Crappie now is found in most eastern and midwestern states and into southern Canada, as well as some waters in western states.

WHERE TO FISH: Lakes, reservoirs and slow-moving rivers. Prefers clean water. Most hold deep, around brush—except during the spring spawning season when they bed in shallow water around grass or other aquatic vegetation.

White Crappie
Pomoxis annularis

OTHER NAMES:

Sac Au Lait
Papermouth
White Perch
Speckled Perch

RANGE: *Like the Black Crappie, it is now found over most of the East and Midwest, from southern Canada to the Gulf, as well as scattered waters of the West, due to transplanting.*

WHERE TO FISH: *White Crappie can handle murkier waters than Blacks, but both species share many waters, especially in the Midwest and Gulf States. Whites tend to suspend in schools, but always very close to cover, which can range from logs to beds of high plants, to brushpiles.*

DESCRIPTION: Looks much like the Black Crappie but is usually distinguishable by an overall lighter appearance, plus the fact that its markings are more symmetrically arranged in vertical bars. If doubt remains, count the spines in the dorsal fin. The White Crappie has six; the Black has seven or eight.

SIZE: Average is probably slightly larger than the Black Crappie. Most weigh around 12 ounces, but 1- to 2-pounders are common, and catches over 3 pounds are always possible. World record 5 pounds, 3 ounces.

FOOD VALUE: Excellent.

GAME QUALITIES: Fun to catch but not really strong.

TACKLE: Poles take plenty of fish in spring when they are in shallow water. Later in the season, spinning tackle is required for easy use in depths of 12 or 15 feet, or sometimes more. Fly fishing can also be productive in the spring.

LURES AND BAITS: Live minnows, trolled or drifted, take the huge majority of White Crappie, followed closely by tiny jigs and spinners, but nearly every kind of artificial can collect a few fish.

Flier

Centrarchus macropterus

DESCRIPTION: Superficially resembles the Crappies because of the many spots on its side and its large dorsal and anal fins. The color is black to gray on top; white or silvery on lower sides and belly.

SIZE: Seldom reaches a pound. Most are well under one-half pound. World record 1 pound, 4 ounces.

FOOD VALUE: Excellent.

GAME QUALITIES: Spunky but small.

TACKLE: Seldom targeted specifically, most are caught on poles; a few on fly and spinning tackle.

LURES AND BAITS: Worms, crickets and grass shrimp work best, but Fliers eagerly take tiny spinners and artificial flies, particularly nymphs.

OTHER NAMES:

Chinquapin
Bream
Flier Perch

RANGE: *The Deep South from Maryland to the Gulf, and north along the Mississippi to southern Illinois.*

WHERE TO FISH: *Fliers like still backwaters, swamps and sloughs—often where the water has high tannic acid content that discourages most other panfish.*

Warmouth

Lepomis gulosus

OTHER NAMES:

Warmouth Perch
Goggle-eye

RANGE: *Found throughout the South and as far west as Oklahoma and New Mexico; also ranges as far north as the Great Lakes and, in the East, to western Pennsylvania.*

WHERE TO FISH: *Warmouth tolerate muddier or more stagnant water than most Sunfish and are common in still sloughs, swamp ponds and backwaters. But they also are caught in clear lakes, usually close to stumps and brush.*

DESCRIPTION: Rather square-shaped and thick-bodied, it is similar to the Rock Bass in appearance. Color is overall dark green or brown, almost black in some waters, with scattered lighter bars or blotches on the sides.

SIZE: Usually around 6 ounces or so. Seldom reaches 1 pound, although a few Warmouth heavier than 2 pounds have been taken. World record 2 pounds, 7 ounces.

FOOD VALUE: Very good.

GAME QUALITIES: Much like a small black bass in aggressiveness and fight.

TACKLE: Pole, spinning gear, fly rod.

LURES AND BAITS: Minnows top the list of natural baits but Warmouth are not at all picky and will take worms and insect baits just as well. Fly rodders often get a lot of action on popping bugs. Jigs and spinners are the most-used artificials, but Warmouth often surprise anglers by slugging bass lures.

Bluegill

Lepomis macrochirus

DESCRIPTION: There is great color variation due to different genetic strains and, to some extent, hybridization with other Sunfish species. Still, the Bluegill usually is not difficult to identify because of its deep, rounded body, dark vertical bars and the solid black flap at the end of the gill cover. The breast is vivid red or yellow in breeding fish, and large specimens show a coppery sheen atop the head. Small Bluegills, especially those from clear water, can be almost colorless.

SIZE: Commonly caught in sizes from a couple of ounces to a half-pound. Fish weighing 8-12 ounces are plentiful at times, especially when bedding. One-pounders are sometimes taken, and some strains can rarely reach as much as 4 pounds. World record 4 pounds, 12 ounces.

FOOD VALUE: Varies from good to excellent. Large fish from still or muddy waters should be skinned for best flavor.

GAME QUALITIES: Though small, it is a hard fighter that uses its broad sides to good advantage against light lines.

TACKLE: Pole, fly rod, spinning gear.

LURES AND BAITS: The Bluegill's natural diet is made up largely of insects and crustaceans, so baits such as worms, crickets and grass shrimp are widely used. But Bluegills will happily swallow almost anything organic, including doughballs, canned corn and bits of bacon. They are predatory too and will attack minnows and a variety of small hard lures, such as little spinners. They make excellent flyfishing targets, hitting both small popping bugs and various sinking flies, mainly nymphs.

OTHER NAMES:

Bream
Blue Bream
Blue Sunfish
Coppernose
Sunny

RANGE: Native to the East and South, Bluegills have been transplanted even more widely than the Largemouth Bass and are now found in most of the lower states and Hawaii, plus southeastern Canada. The species is especially popular for stocking in new lakes and farm ponds.

WHERE TO FISH: Equally at home in lakes, ponds and streams, the Bluegill likes to hang close to grass, lily pads and shorelines but often wanders to deep, open water.

Pumpkinseed

Lepomis gibbosus

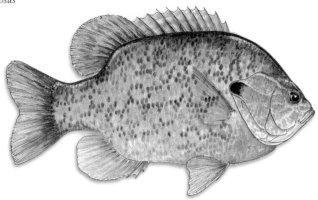

OTHER NAMES:

Common Sunfish Sunny

RANGE: *From the Midwest across the Great Lakes region and into southeastern Canada, then southward to South Carolina. Widely introduced farther west and now found from the Dakotas and southern Ontario to the Pacific Coast and Rocky Mountain areas.*

WHERE TO FISH: *Mostly lakes and ponds, but also found in slow streams. Pumpkinseeds hug the shoreline and so should those fishing for them. They love to hang around docks, ramps and shoreline weed patches.*

DESCRIPTION: Less variation than with the Bluegill. The body is greenish and marked with wavy lines and orange spots. The black gill flap is tipped with red. Several blue lines extend from the mouth across the cheek and gill cover.

SIZE: Often 4 to 10 ounces. One-pounders are rare. World record 1 pound, 6 ounces.

FOOD VALUE: Excellent.

GAME QUALITIES: Fun but not a challenge.

TACKLE: Pole, fly rod, ultralight spinning.

LURES AND BAITS: The majority fall to pole fishermen using worms for bait. Grubs and other larvae are excellent too. In spring, dry flies and small sinking flies can get a lot of action. Tiny spinners and jigs will catch some Pumpkinseeds, but spin fishermen mostly stick to natural bait fished on bottom or below a float. Like Bluegill, Pumpkinseeds will hit bread and many other delicacies not included in their natural diets.

Redear Sunfish

Lepomis microlophus

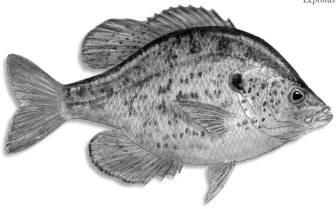

DESCRIPTION: A bright red spot at the end of the gill flap sets it apart. It also is less round than most other Sunfish and, usually, larger. Color is olive or bluish on the sides with a bright yellow belly. Markings on the sides are variable, but often take the form of dark vertical bars.

SIZE: The average is more than a half-pound, and fish weighing around 1 pound are fairly common. Two-pounders are not rare, and the potential is to as much as 4 pounds or so. World record 5 pounds, 7 ounces.

FOOD VALUE: Excellent; produces thick and tasty fillets.

GAME QUALITIES: Partly because of size it is a tough customer on light line.

TACKLE: Pole, spinning gear, fly rod.

LURES AND BAITS: Mollusks make up a good portion of its natural diet, hence the name "Shellcracker," used in much of the South. Anglers, however, tend to use earthworms and poles to fish spawning beds. Worms fished near the bottom are most productive. Flyrod anglers do especially well with spinner-fly combinations.

OTHER NAMES:

**Shellcracker
Yellow Bream**

RANGE: *Mostly the Deep South. Extends as far north as Virginia on the coast and to Illinois and Indiana in the heartland. To the west, it is found in Oklahoma and Texas, and has been introduced into scattered other areas, although not nearly so widely as the Bluegill.*

WHERE TO FISH: *Most fishing for Redears takes place in shallow, weedy water during the spring bedding season. Many are caught at other times, but are difficult to target then and usually turn up in mixed bags with other kinds of panfish.*

Redbreast Sunfish

Lepomis auritus

OTHER NAMES:

Sun Perch
Redbelly
River Bream
Robin Perch
Yellowbelly

RANGE: *Native to the East Coast states and southern New Brunswick. Introduced into other southern states as far west as Texas.*

WHERE TO FISH: *The Redbreast likes flowing water and is nearly always found in rivers and creeks or lakes directly fed by streams.*

DESCRIPTION: Color is light or dark blue above; yellowish on sides. The breast is bright red in adult males; yellow in females. Wavy lines mark the gill covers. The long, narrow gill flap is solid black.

SIZE: Averages 4-8 ounces. Usual maximum is about 1 pound. World record 1 pound, 12 ounces.

FOOD VALUE: Excellent; best of the Sunfish.

GAME QUALITIES: Aggressive striker and strong battler for its size.

TACKLE: Pole, spinning tackle, fly gear.

LURES AND BAITS: Crickets and larvae may work best, but worms do good work too. Redbreast often attack bass-size plugs, but spin fishermen catch many more on small in-line spinners and grub-tipped spinnerbaits. Popping bugs and flies work well too, particularly nymphs and wet flies.

Spotted Sunfish

Lepomis punctatus

DESCRIPTION: The back and sides are dark, with the belly usually cream colored or pale red. Liberally peppered with small black dots.

SIZE: Few reach one-half pound and the largest are less than a pound.

FOOD VALUE: Excellent.

GAME QUALITIES: Possibly the most aggressive of the Sunfish, but size keeps its fight from equaling its attitude.

TACKLE: Pole, fly rod, spinning gear.

LURES AND BAITS: Nothing beats earthworms dangled around stumps, but this little fellow will dash from hiding to hit nearly any small bait, lure or flyrod popper.

OTHER NAMES:

Stumpknocker

RANGE: *Most of the Southeast from Texas to Florida, then northward to North Carolina. Also in the Mississippi basin north to Illinois.*

WHERE TO FISH: *Likes still water, where it hugs tightly under ledges and limbs, or around snags and stumps.*

Longear Sunfish

Lepomis megalotis

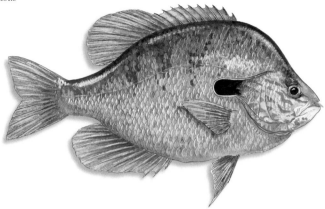

OTHER NAMES:

Bigear
Redbellied Bream

RANGE: *From the Florida Panhandle north to the Great Lakes and west to New Mexico. Absent from most of Florida and the Atlantic Coast states.*

WHERE TO FISH: *Like the Redbreast it prefers flowing streams, preferably the upper reaches where water is swifter and clear. Has adapted to reservoirs in some areas.*

DESCRIPTION: Very similar in appearance to the Redbreast. Sides are brassy with patches and streaks of blue. The belly is bright yellow to orange. The gill flap is long and black but, unlike that of the Redbreast, is bordered in blue.

SIZE: Slightly smaller on average than the Redbreast. A big one will weigh 8 or 9 ounces. World record 1 pound, 12 ounces.

FOOD VALUE: Excellent.

GAME QUALITIES: Strong battler for its size.

TACKLE: Pole, fly rod, ultralight spinning.

LURES AND BAITS: Worms, larvae and crickets top a long list of good natural baits. Flyrod poppers and tiny topwater spinning plugs are also excellent, as are wet flies and little spinners.

Green Sunfish

Lepomis cyanellus

DESCRIPTION: More like the Warmouth than like other Sunfish because of its chunky silhouette and large mouth. Color is olive green with gold flecks and light vertical bars. Green lines on cheek and gill cover. Dark spots at rear base of dorsal and anal fins.

SIZE: Averages 4-8 ounces. Even though 1-pounders are rare, 2-pounders are on record. World record 2 pounds, 2 ounces.

FOOD VALUE: Very good.

GAME QUALITIES: Well liked more because they are cooperative than for their fighting ability.

TACKLE: Pole, light spinning, fly.

LURES AND BAITS: Most are caught with worms, crickets, larvae or tiny minnows as bait, but they will hit popping bugs, artificial flies and small spinners.

OTHER NAMES:

Sunny
Greeny
Green Perch
Sand Bass
Rubbertail

RANGE: *From the Appalachians west to New Mexico and Colorado; and from the Gulf states (except Florida) to the Great Lakes and into southern Ontario. Introduced to various other areas.*

WHERE TO FISH: *Greenies prefer still water—lakes, ponds and backwaters of streams. They usually are found close to vegetation or snags.*

The Striped Bass ranks among the elite game species of both saltwater and freshwater anglers in America. The freshwater portion of the fishery takes place in two major arenas—various streams of the Atlantic, Gulf and Pacific coasts where Stripers spawn; plus impoundments in nearly every part of the country, where fish bred and stocked by conservation agencies thrive and grow to often huge size. They are unable to reproduce, however, in most of their landlocked homes, so must be regularly restocked. The White Bass is a small freshwater cousin of the Striper that shares many of its attributes. Mix the two together—as government hatcheries often do—and you get a crossbreed known in Florida as the Sunshine Bass and everywhere else as either the Whiterock Bass, Wiper, or simply, "Hybrid." It is easily raised and replenished in great number, and while it does not attain so huge a size as the Striper, it does grow far larger than its other parent, the White Bass. Overall, Hybrids are hardier and more adaptable than Stripers, and for that reason are chosen for planting in a greater variety of waters. Two other small species in this group are the Yellow Bass, a popular panfish in the Mississippi basin and other parts of the Midwest, and the familiar White Perch, which, despite its common name, is a bona fide member of the "Temperate Basses," as this family is referred to by biologists.

Chapter

The Striped Basses

Hybrid Bass
Striped Bass
White Bass
White Perch
Yellow Bass

Hybrid Bass

Morone saxatilis x M. chrysops

OTHER NAMES:

Whiterock Bass
Sunshine Bass
Cherokee Bass
Wiper

RANGE: *Strictly a hatchery fish, the Hybrid has no natural range, but is widely stocked by state fishery departments, particularly in the South. Check with your state's fishery agency or license outlet to find out if they are available, and in which waters.*

WHERE TO FISH: *Like its two parents, the Hybrid stays deep much of the time, but offers fast casting action when schooling at the surface. When deep, try vertical jigging or livebait fishing around brushpiles and dropoffs, or around bends in rivers.*

DESCRIPTION: This hybrid of the Striped and White Basses is similar in appearance to both. They are most easily distinguished by the stripes, which usually are broken and irregular. Hybrids have two parallel tooth patches on their tongues while white bass have a single round patch. Also, many waters stocked with Hybrids do not contain the other species, eliminating the chance for confusion.

SIZE: Commonly reaches 8 or 10 pounds; sometimes exceeds 15 pounds. World record 27 pounds, 5 ounces.

FOOD VALUE: Very good.

GAME QUALITIES: Outstanding; not easy to fool and a terrific battler.

TACKLE: Light spinning and baitcasting.

LURES AND BAITS: Spoons and shad-imitating plugs and jigs. Shiners, shad and minnows are productive natural baits.

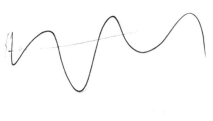

Striped Bass

Morone saxatilis

DESCRIPTION: Heavy-bodied with long head and underslung jaw. Color typically is dark green to dark gray above, silvery on the sides and belly. Seven or eight longitudinal stripes, regularly spaced and usually unbroken, mark the sides.

SIZE: Reaches 50 pounds or more, but most catches run 5-20 pounds. World record 78 pounds, 8 ounces from salt water, freshwater record 67.8 pounds.

FOOD VALUE: Very good. The flesh is light and rich.

GAME QUALITIES: Stubborn and very strong, the Striper is a tough challenge for the angler, particularly where strong currents are involved.

TACKLE: For deep trolling and live-baiting, stout bait-casting and spinning rods and reels with large line capacity. For shallow fishing, lighter versions of the same gear, plus medium to heavy fly tackle.

LURES AND BAITS: Trolling plugs and spoons for deep fishing; spoons, topwater plugs, and shallow crankbaits for surface and shallow casting. Productive flies include large poppers and streamers that resemble shad.

OTHER NAMES:

Striper
Rockfish
Rockbass
Greenhead

RANGE: Natural runs of this anadromous species occur in rivers of the Atlantic Coast from New Brunswick to North Florida, and on the Gulf Coast from the Florida Panhandle to the Mississippi River. Successfully introduced to San Francisco Bay in 1879, it now is reported along the Pacific Coast from southern California to Vancouver, B.C., although it remains most plentiful in the San Francisco area. Stripers also thrive in landlocked fresh water, and stocking programs have achieved consistent sport fisheries in many reservoirs and several river systems as far west as the Colorado River.

WHERE TO FISH: In reservoirs, Stripers stay deep most of the time and are best fished by trolling or drifting with live baits. Surface activity often takes place, however, when the Bass attack schooling shad. Opportunistic anglers then can cast for them with artificial lures and sometimes flies. In rivers, Stripers like areas where deep, running water sweeps past shallow points; also eddies, bars and creek runoffs.

White Bass

Morone chrysops

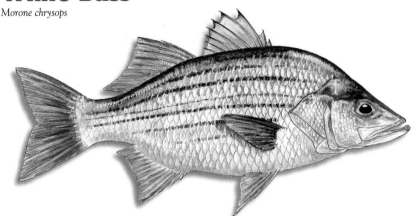

OTHER NAMES:

Silver Bass
Striper

RANGE: *White Bass thrive in large reservoirs, but also are found in big rivers and some large natural lakes.*

WHERE TO FISH: *Although White Bass are caught "blind" by casting in runoffs, below dams or around points where fast currents and eddies combine to provide a good feeding station, best fishing occurs during largely unpredictable times when they school at the surface to attack baitfish. The White Bass "run" concentrates fish in the spring, often below dams.*

DESCRIPTION: Due to transplanting, now found in most of the East, Southeast and Midwest and many areas in the Southwest. Also in lower Canada from Quebec west to Manitoba.

SIZE: Usually a pound or so but can top 5 pounds on occasion. World record 6 pounds, 13 ounces.

FOOD VALUE: Good. Smaller specimens are tastier.

GAME QUALITIES: Hard striker and strong fighter for its size.

TACKLE: Light spinning and baitcasting; also fly gear.

LURES AND BAITS: Small surface plugs and crankbaits; spoons, jigs, popping bugs and streamer flies that imitate shad. Minnows and other small baitfish are top natural baits.

Yellow Bass
Morone mississippiensis

DESCRIPTION: Outline similar to White Bass, but body is slenderer and the sides are yellow or brassy in color, often tinged with green. Stripes generally unbroken above the lateral line but interrupted below.

SIZE: Smaller on average than the White, most weigh one-half pound or less. World record 2 pounds, 9 ounces.

FOOD VALUE: Excellent.

GAME QUALITIES: Tough little fighters.

TACKLE: Spinning, baitcasting and fly.

LURES AND BAITS: Natural baits and sinking plugs.

OTHER NAMES:

Barfish
Brassy Bass
Streaker

RANGE: *Found only in the Mississippi River drainage from Minnesota to Louisiana, thence eastward to Mobile Bay and westward to East Texas.*

WHERE TO FISH: *Inhabits both streams and lakes.*

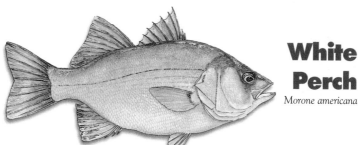

White Perch
Morone americana

DESCRIPTION: A perch in name only. Vaguely similar to the related White Bass, the White Perch loses its stripes by adulthood.

SIZE: Most weigh less than a pound. World record 4 pounds, 12 ounces.

FOOD VALUE: Excellent.

GAME QUALITIES: Very spirited despite small size.

TACKLE: Ultralight spinning, pole, light fly tackle.

LURES AND BAITS: Not choosy and feed heavily on insects and crustaceans as well as small fish.

OTHER NAMES:

Sea Perch
Narrow-mouthed Bass

RANGE: *Atlantic Provinces and states from Nova Scotia to North Carolina. Has entered the Great Lakes.*

WHERE TO FISH: *An extremely popular panfish, it roams far upstream but the best Perch fishing takes place in the lower reaches of rivers.*

Yes, the Walleye is a Perch, not a Pike—a fact that's well known to most devoted Walleye fishermen, if still not quite clear to non-anglers who know the fish only by its well deserved culinary reputation. And don't let the Walleye's glassy stare fool you, either. Its vision is plenty good enough to zero in on the many thousands of jigs, spinners, plugs and natural baits offered to it by Walleye seekers from Canada's far North all the way to the Deep South of the United States. Walleye fishermen, in fact, rival bass anglers in number over much of the country. A smaller species that's sometimes confused with the Walleye is the Sauger—but note that the Walleye's tail is tipped in white while the Sauger's is not. One other member of this group also commands a huge following. That, of course, is the Yellow Perch, a tasty panfish that is a favorite across a broad spectrum of interests, from juvenile fishermen dabbling baits in neighborhood ponds to ice fishermen. All the other species covered in this section are familiar but seldom fished for, except to serve as bait for larger fish. Many waders and swimmers know the Darters, having seen them dart many times from a place of hiding under one rock to a new haven under another.

Perches & Pseudo Perches

Walleye

Sauger

Yellow Perch

Logperch

Johnny Darter

Tule Perch

Trout-perch

Pirate Perch

Walleye
Stizostedion vitreum

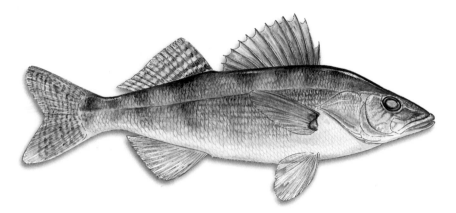

OTHER NAMES:

Walleyed Pike
Pike-perch
Yellow Pike
Pickerel
Dore'

RANGE: *A hardy, adaptable species, the Walleye has been widely introduced and now is found throughout most of sub-arctic Canada and in all mainland states except Alaska, Maine, Delaware, California and Florida.*

WHERE TO FISH: *With rare exceptions, Walleyes feed near bottom in both lakes and large, fairly slow rivers. They do orient to structure, such as brush and bars, but sometimes are found over bare bottom when bait schools are present. Walleye hit best when light is low—early, late and after dark.*

DESCRIPTION: The elongated body is overall greenish or brown in color, with darker blotches along the side and a white belly. Eyes are large and glassy. There is a dark spot at rear of its forward dorsal fin. Lower lobes of the anal fin and tail are tipped in white. Mouth is large and has prominent canine teeth.

SIZE: Largest North American member of the perch family, the Walleye not infrequently tops 8 pounds, and can exceed 20 pounds, but most catches are 1 to 4 pounds. World record 25 pounds.

FOOD VALUE: Widely regarded as among the best of all freshwater fish.

GAME QUALITIES: The fight is strong but rather short-lived.

TACKLE: Spinning and baitcasting gear; seldom an attractive flyfishing target.

LURES AND BAITS: Minnows, leeches and night-crawlers are the most frequently chosen natural baits. Both work well alone but are often even more productive in combination with spinners. Among artificial lures, jigs are perhaps the most widely effective, although Walleyes, like Bass, will at times hit nearly any lure. Other particularly good ones are in-line spinners and crankbaits. Slow-trolling of crankbaits, especially the slender minnow designs, is a good approach in reasonably shallow water.

Sauger
Stizostedion canadense

DESCRIPTION: Almost a dead ringer for the Walleye—but not quite. The Sauger is easily differentiated by the numerous small spots on the forward dorsal fin. Also, the anal and lower tail fins of the Walleye are tipped in white. The similar **Saugeye, Stizostedian vitreum x S. canadense,** is a hybrid hatchery fish crossing a Walleye and Sauger to produce a very popular sportfish in the rivers and streams of Ohio and many other areas.

SIZE: The usual Sauger catch weighs a pound or so, and a 3-pounder is a lunker. World record 8 pounds, 12 ounces.

FOOD VALUE: Excellent.

GAME QUALITIES: Like a walleye but smaller.

TACKLE: Spinning and baitcasting.

LURES AND BAITS: Minnows, worms, jigs and spinners are probably the best producers. Like the Walleye, however, a Sauger might turn up on just about any lure an angler tosses into the water.

OTHER NAMES:

Sand Pickerel
Sand Pike
River Pike
Gray Pike
Jack Salmon

RANGE: *Like the Walleye, the Sauger has been widely transplanted and thrives in reservoirs and big natural lakes. Its range is more limited to central and eastern North America.*

WHERE TO FISH: *By far the most frantic fishing takes place in the tailwaters of major dams in the central and the southern states during winter and early spring. Otherwise, Sauger have much the same habits as Walleye and are often caught incidental to Walleye fishing.*

Yellow Perch

Perca flavescens

OTHER NAMES:

Lake Perch
American Perch
Ringed Perch
Striped Perch
Jack Perch

RANGE: *Much of Lower Canada, from the Northwest Territories and Manitoba eastward to Nova Scotia. In the States, it is most plentiful from Minnesota to New England, but is found as far south as Georgia, and has been introduced to many scattered areas of the country.*

WHERE TO FISH: *Yellow Perch prefer clear ponds and lakes but are also found in rivers. They like cover close to shore and so make great targets for nearly anyone who can reach the water. Most bites occur just off the bottom.*

DESCRIPTION: The sides are yellow. The back is dark olive, as are several wide dark bars that mark the sides. The tail is slightly forked.

SIZE: Most weigh under a pound, although specimens up to 2 pounds sometimes fall to a lucky angler. The potential maximum is 4 pounds or slightly more. World record 4 pounds, 3 ounces.

FOOD VALUE: Very good.

GAME QUALITIES: Spirited on light tackle.

TACKLE: Pole, light and ultralight spinning tackle, fly rod.

LURES AND BAITS: Like Sunfish and other panfish, Yellow Perch will eat a wide variety of baits, but earthworms and small minnows are as good as any. They also hit tiny jigs and spinners, and sunken flies.

Logperch

Percina caprodes

DESCRIPTION: This is one of the largest and most widely distributed of the Darter group of species. It is brownish above with a string of alternating long and short bars extending its full length. They have bulbous, upturned noses that they use for rooting out food from the bottom.

SIZE: This species reaches about 8 inches; others perhaps 5 or 6 inches.

FOOD VALUE: Poor.

GAME QUALITIES: Poor.

TACKLE: Pole, fly rod.

LURES AND BAITS: Small insects and flies, natural or artificial.

OTHER NAMES:

Common Logperch
Bignose Darter

RANGE: All Logperch species are found east of the Rockies. The common type ranges through most of the East, from the Gulf to the Great Lakes, and in Canada from Quebec to Saskatchewan.

WHERE TO FISH: Small to medium streams, in riffles and rocky runs. Not fished for, except perhaps by children, but sometimes caught on wet flies and nymphs while trout fishing.

Johnny Darter

Etheostoma nigrum

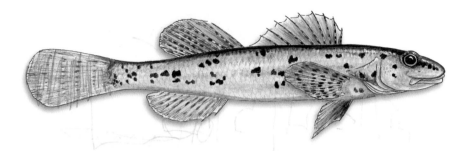

RANGE: *The Johnny Darter is found in most of the East and Midwest and into Lower Canada. Many of the other Darter species have very limited distribution, but as a group they blanket the country and Canada, from the Rockies to the Atlantic.*

WHERE TO FISH: *All Darters stick smack on the bottom, hiding among rocks and twigs. They never swim around freely but dart swiftly from spot to spot. Anglers sometimes chase them into nets for use as bait.*

DESCRIPTION: This fish, the Johnny Darter, is chosen to represent a large group of Darters that are common over much of the country yet not commonly noted. The Johnny Darter is brown to tan with several saddle marks on the dorsal surface and numerous X marks on the side.

SIZE: No more than 2 or 3 inches.

FOOD VALUE: Nil.

GAME QUALITIES: None.

TACKLE: Dipnet or small seine.

LURES AND BAITS: None effective, although an occasional Darter is taken on a trout fly.

Tule Perch

Hysterocarpus traski

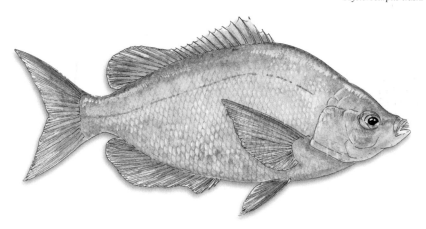

DESCRIPTION: This is the only inland species of the surf perches. Compressed body is blue above with white or dull yellow sides marked by dark bars and scattered oblique lines. Small mouth, round body and somewhat forked tail.

SIZE: Maximum about 8 inches.

FOOD VALUE: Not bad but not much there.

GAME QUALITIES: No gamester but a good target for youthful anglers.

TACKLE: Pole.

LURES AND BAITS: Small insects, bits of worm or shrimp.

RANGE: Northern California—mainly Sacramento River and tributaries, plus Russian River and Clear Lake.

WHERE TO FISH: Close to emergent vegetation.

Trout-perch

Percopsis omiscomaycus

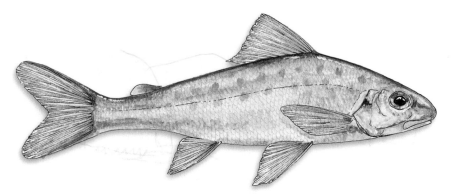

RANGE: *From Potomac and Delaware River drainages north to Quebec, west to Ohio and Missouri River drainages, and north through most of western Canada to Alaska.*

WHERE TO FISH: *Lakes, ponds and slow-moving streams. Typically stays deep during the day, feeding in evening and at night in the shallows and along shorelines.*

DESCRIPTION: Head is large and unscaled. Color is transparent yellow with white specks. Dorsal fin is large and triangular; tail is forked. Adipose fin is present.

SIZE: Grows to about 8 inches.

FOOD VALUE: Minimal.

GAME QUALITIES: Sometimes sought for fun by children, but generally used for bait.

TACKLE: Pole, dipnet. Also caught incidentally by fly fishermen.

LURES AND BAITS: Worms or any sort of insect life; many kinds of artificial flies.

Pirate Perch

Aphredoderus sayanus

DESCRIPTION: Unique in that the urogenitals of adults are located in the throat region on the underside of the head. The body is short and deep and the head and mouth are large. Color is dark gray above and yellowish below. Large specimens are often purple-hued. Dorsal and tail fins are large and rounded.

SIZE: To about 6 inches.

FOOD VALUE: Minimal.

GAME QUALITIES: No food value but good bait.

TACKLE: Pole, dipnet.

LURES AND BAITS: Bits of worm and small insects.

RANGE: From Florida north to New York and west to the Appalachians; also the Gulf States and the Mississippi River valley north to the Great Lakes.

WHERE TO FISH: Lakes, ponds and slow streams with good vegetation. Rarely strays far from cover.

All Pike species share an unmistakable family resemblance, with their proportionately slender shapes, long, toothy jaws and bountiful sharp teeth. What sets them apart is size. King of the clan is the gigantic and spectacular Muskellunge, nearly always called Muskie—and spelled either Muskie or Musky. For many years it has enjoyed the reputation of being a stubborn target that requires hundreds, perhaps even thousands of casts before its anger can be provoked into striking. That scenario is indeed valid in many hard-fished waters, but modern Muskie fishermen, thanks to the compiled past experiences of their many predecessors, combined with access to a great deal of "new" Muskie territory that was unknown, or almost unreachable, just a few decades ago, have greatly shortened the interval between strikes. While catching a Muskie will always remain a great challenge, it is now at least a reasonable challenge for anyone with desire and a little extra patience. And for those who don't care to wait at all, there is the Northern Pike, a close but much more cooperative relative of the Muskie that is widely distributed throughout most of Canada and the northern States. The Northern is virtually the Muskie's equal in all attributes except maximum size. The Tiger Musky is a cross between the Muskellunge and Northern that is produced sometimes by nature but far more often in government fish hatcheries. Working down the scale, the small Chain Pickerel is familiar to many anglers that never get to see any of the giant Pike species. It is a fine battler itself, but without much heft to back up its attitude. The remaining member of the clan is the Redfin Pickerel, or Grass Pickerel, which is smaller still and barely capable of bending a light rod, yet nevertheless exhibits the characteristic family aggressiveness.

The Pikes

Muskellunge

Tiger Muskellunge

Northern Pike

Chain Pickerel

Redfin Pickerel

Muskellunge

Esox masquinongy

OTHER NAMES:

Musky
Muskie
Maskinonge
Great Pike

RANGE: *From the St. Lawrence Waterway westward through the Great Lakes and Canadian border area to eastern Manitoba; southward from the St. Lawrence to Tennessee and western North Carolina.*

WHERE TO FISH: *Muskies are solitary fish that like to lurk in, or on the edge of, weedbeds, but in hot weather they go deep, usually orienting to ledges and other submerged structure. They also are found in rivers, generally lurking in slow bends or eddying pools close to logs or weedbeds. A Muskie will take up residence in a particular spot and can be cast to numerous times before making up its mind to strike.*

DESCRIPTION: Color is variable but the back is often dark gray to green. Yellowish sides have variable markings, the three most common being barred, spotted and plain. Tips of the forked tail are pointed. Like all the Pikes, the Muskie has a long, underslung jaw and plenty of sharp teeth. The underside of the jaw shows a series of pores, more than five on each side.

SIZE: Largest of the Pikes, the Muskie is common at 15-30 pounds and can reach 40, 50, even 60 pounds or more. However, many catches fall in the neighborhood of 8-14 pounds. World record 67 pounds, 8 ounces.

FOOD VALUE: Very good but most are released.

GAME QUALITIES: One of the toughest of freshwater fish. The fight is vicious and showy, and can include some spectacular leaping.

TACKLE: Stout baitcasting gear is best, but spinning tackle is often used. Stout fly rods fill the bill too, but fly casting for Muskie takes more patience than most anglers can muster.

LURES AND BAITS: Top natural baits are live or rigged Suckers and other fish. Large and noisy topwater plugs, hefty jerkbaits and bucktail spinners lead the list of productive lures. Large diving plugs, heavy spoons and live baits are trolled or drifted for deep fish. A few adventurous fly fishermen go after Muskie with streamer flies five or six inches long.

Tiger Muskellunge

Esox lucius x E. masquinongy

DESCRIPTION: This hybrid of the Northern Pike and Muskellunge has a dark, tiger-stripe pattern on a light background, much like the barred phase of the Muskie but the stripes usually are more vivid. The tips of the tail fin are rounded. Pores on the underside of the jaw number five to seven on each side.

SIZE: Generally averages smaller than the Muskie—but not by much. Many 15- to 20-pound fish are taken and a few specimens top 40 pounds. World record 51 pounds, 3 ounces.

FOOD VALUE: Very good, but most are released.

GAME QUALITIES: Strong, rugged brawler, with lots of surface show.

TACKLE: Stout baitcasting and spinning gear; some anglers try fly tackle.

LURES AND BAITS: Splashy topwater plugs, spinners and spoons are the best lures. Live suckers and other large baitfish top the list of natural baits.

OTHER NAMES:

Tiger Musky
Hybrid Musky

RANGE: *Basically the same as the Muskellunge, but because it is easier to raise it probably has been introduced more widely, especially in the South. Some natural hyridization takes place too.*

WHERE TO FISH: *Around logs, snags and weedbeds; eddying pools in rivers—same habitat as for the Muskie.*

Northern Pike

Esox lucius

OTHER NAMES:

Northern Pickerel Jack Jackfish

RANGE: *Alaska, most of Canada, the U.S. border states, and south to Nebraska and Missouri.*

WHERE TO FISH: *Like the Muskies, Northerns tend to lurk in and around weedbeds and logs or ledges but, unlike Muskies, they are often eager to attack baits and lures thrown their way.*

DESCRIPTION: Dark green on top and lighter green on sides, with yellowish belly. Numerous bean-shaped yellow spots dot the sides, with darker markings on dorsal and anal fins. The tail is slightly forked and the tips are round. Pores on underside of jaw number five or more.

SIZE: Common at 4-10 pounds and frequently tops 20 pounds. The potential maximum is more than 30 pounds. World record 55 pounds, 1 ounce (from Germany). North American record 46 pounds, 2 ounces.

FOOD VALUE: Very good.

GAME QUALITIES: A savage fighter that runs, thrashes and jumps.

TACKLE: Baitcasting, spinning and fly all have devotees. Northerns respond well to speedily retrieved flies.

LURES AND BAITS: All kinds of small live fish are excellent. Topping a long list of productive lures are spoons, spinners, jigs, topwater plugs and, for fly fishing, very large streamers and poppers. With any lure, bright colors usually produce more strikes.

Chain Pickerel
Esox niger

DESCRIPTION: Coloration is green on top and lighter on the sides, which have chain-like markings. The tail is forked and the lobes pointed.

SIZE Most run 1-2 pounds. Although the maximum is around 9 pounds, a 4-pounder is considered a lunker anywhere. World record 9 pounds, 6 ounces.

FOOD VALUE: Excellent taste but very bony.

GAME QUALITIES: A fine battler for its size. Strikes viciously and gets off spirited runs and thrashing jumps.

TACKLE: Any sort of bass tackle.

LURES AND BAITS: Pickerel will hit the entire gamut of bass lures, but have a special fondness for spinners and spoons.

OTHER NAMES:

Eastern Pickerel
Lake Pickerel
Jack
Pike

RANGE: *Atlantic Provinces and states from New Brunswick and Nova Scotia south to Florida. Also Alabama and the Mississippi basin north to southern Missouri, Kentucky and Illinois. Scattered introductions elsewhere.*

WHERE TO FISH: *Weedbeds, lily pads and snags, especially in still, backwater areas.*

Redfin Pickerel
Esox americanus americanus

DESCRIPTION: Bars mark the sides, instead of the chain-like pattern of the Chain Pickerel. The snout is also shorter and comparatively wider, and the fins are red.

SIZE: Most are under a foot long. A rare one will top 1 pound. World record 2 pounds, 4 ounces.

FOOD VALUE: Excellent though bony.

GAME QUALITIES: Too small to resist very much.

TACKLE: Pole, light spinning.

LURES AND BAITS: Minnows, strips of fish, pork rind, small weedless lures.

OTHER NAMES:

Grass Pickerel

RANGE: *Same territory as the Chain Pickerel, plus wider distribution in the Midwest, where it extends north to the Great Lakes states and west to East Texas, Oklahoma, Kansas and Nebraska.*

WHERE TO FISH: *Mostly small ponds, slow creeks and very shallow, grassy edges of larger lakes and streams.*

T hese are the glamour species of cold-water fishing, but identification of the many species of Trouts, Salmons and Chars can be a difficult proposition, sometimes even for fishermen with considerable experience. As for newcomers to the sport— well, they will probably find the task truly daunting. For one thing, many of the Salmons are alike in superficial coloration, being mostly silver. Add to that the fact that several species of sea-run Trout and Char are also silver—for a while, at least, until their color begins to return upriver. And that hints at another problem. Whether sea-run or not, individuals of the more brightly hued members of the family tend to vary a great deal in coloration, these variations being due to a number of factors that include sex, size, season, diet and environment. Just separating the Trouts from the Salmons from the Chars is no easy task in itself, because popular names have long been arbitrary and confusing. For instance, the Brook Trout and Lake Trout actually belong to the Char genus; the Rainbow and Cutthroat Trouts are grouped scientifically with the Pacific Salmons; and the Atlantic Salmon is a biological brother to the Brown Trout. Scientists avoid confusion by referring to all of them as Salmonids. Certain physical characteristics of each species are more reliable identifiers than color, and these are noted in the descriptions that follow. Regardless of classification, however, all Salmonids—from six-inch Brookies in mountain streams to huge Salmon and Rainbows in big lakes and rivers— are gamefish of the very highest stature.

Trouts, Salmons, & Chars

Arctic Char

Brook Trout

Lake Trout

Dolly Varden

Bull Trout

Atlantic Salmon

Landlocked Salmon

Brown Trout

Rainbow Trout

Steelhead

Cutthroat Trout

Golden Trout

Chinook Salmon

Coho Salmon

Sockeye Salmon

Kokanee Salmon

Chum Salmon

Pink Salmon

Arctic Char

Salvelinus alpinus

OTHER NAMES:

Blueback Char

RANGE: *The northernmost of all sportfish, it ranges from northern Quebec and Newfoundland to Baffin Island on the Atlantic Coast, thence across arctic and subarctic Canada to Alaska. Landlocked populations are found in some New England waters as well.*

WHERE TO FISH: *Schools hold in deep areas of rivers and lakes, but feed actively in shallow riffles. Sea-run Char are fishable from shore in river mouths and estuaries of the far North.*

DESCRIPTION: Sea-run fish are silver, usually with pale whitish or pinkish dots, although dots may be absent. Upriver and in lakes many specimens are greenish or brownish above, with pink to orange or deep red below. Colors are most vivid in spawning males. If present, dots on the sides are usually white or red. There are no markings on the dorsal fin or tail, which is slightly forked.

SIZE: Averages 2 or 3 pounds. Fish up to 10 pounds are not unusual in many areas, particularly among sea-run Char, and the potential is to more than 25 pounds. World record 32 pounds, 9 ounces.

FOOD VALUE: Very good in fresh-run and landlocked fish but quality deteriorates as spawning fish progress upriver.

GAME QUALITIES: Hard striker and good runner but, like other salmonids, the anadromous fish lose muscle tone and strength after considerable time in the rivers.

TACKLE: Since Char prefer to feed on small baitfish, spinning or light baitcasting gear will outdo fly tackle in most environments, but they do feed on insects as well, and fly fishing is often practical and productive.

LURES AND BAITS: Flashy spoons and spinners are best hard lures everywhere. Minnow-imitating streamers are the best choice for fly fishing during early runs, but wet flies and nymph patterns work very well in lakes and also in rivers after the runs have had time to settle in. Success with dry flies is apt to be sporadic and unpredictable.

Brook Trout

Salvelinus fontinalis

DESCRIPTION: Similar in shape to the Arctic Char but distinguishable by the wormlike pattern on the upper sides, dorsal fin and caudal fin. Color is usually olive to black above, shading to gray on underside and belly, except in breeding males, which sport bright red underparts. In addition to the vermiculated markings, red spots with blue halos are generally present.

SIZE: In small streams the average is less than a pound, with 2-pounders being rare and praiseworthy south of Maine. Very big Brookies are caught, frequently in some areas, notably northern Quebec and Labrador. There, 5-pounders are fairly common and the potential is to more than 10 pounds. World record 14 pounds, 8 ounces.

FOOD VALUE: Excellent.

GAME QUALITIES: Pound-for-pound (or even ounce-for-ounce), Brookies rank among the best. The fight is strong and showy, even though jumps are rare.

TACKLE: Although spinning and even baitcasting outfits are frequently used in larger waters of the North Country for big fish, the Brookie is a textbook fly fish, and the pet of most old-time fly rodders in the East.

LURES AND BAITS: A long list of natural baits includes worms, grasshoppers, minnows and leeches. Small spinners and spoons are tops as hard lures. All categories of artificial flies also get much play, with dries producing well at the right times. Over most of the season, however, nymphs and terrestrials will probably take the most Brookies, and streamers the largest.

OTHER NAMES:

Brookie
Squaretail
Native Trout
Speckled Trout
Mountain Trout
Salter

RANGE: *Native to eastern North America from Labrador to North Georgia and westward to the Great Lakes States and Manitoba, it has been transplanted to many western waters, even Alaska. It is now prominent in some of the Rocky Mountain States.*

WHERE TO FISH: *Brookies like their streams cleaner and colder than other popular trout or char species. Sea-run fish— "Salters"—are common in some New England and Canadian rivers.*

Lake Trout

Salvelinus namaycush

OTHER NAMES:

Mackinaw
Gray Trout
Laker
Togue
Siscowet

RANGE: Native to most of Canada and many lakes in Alaska and the northernmost Lower States, from coast to coast. Very popular in New England, New York and the Great Lakes. It also has been successfully introduced to a few waters south of its natural range.

WHERE TO FISH: Very deep and very cold lakes; sometimes in tributary rivers.

DESCRIPTION: The body, dorsal and tail fins of most Lakers are brown or dark green and liberally marked with white or yellowish spots. The other fins are usually unmarked and lined with white. The tail is sharply forked. In a few lakes, adult fish may be light in overall color and without noticeable markings.

SIZE: Recorded to more than 100 pounds, the Lake Trout usually runs from about 5 to 30 pounds, occasionally topping 60. World record 72 pounds.

FOOD VALUE: Excellent.

GAME QUALITIES: A strong fighter, although not spectacular or showy.

TACKLE: During short periods of spring and summer (and all summer long in many far northern lakes), Lakers roam shallow water and are fishable with all sorts of casting tackle, including fly rods. Generally, however, they are sought by trolling very deep with heavy baitcasting or spinning tackle, using downriggers or wire line.

LURES AND BAITS: In the shallows, spoons, large spinners and big streamer flies all produce, along with a variety of casting plugs. Deep-trollers rely heavily on spoons, diving plugs and live small fish.

Dolly Varden
Salvelinus malma

DESCRIPTION: Very similar to the Arctic Char and, like the Char, variable in color. Sea-run fish are usually silvery with pale blue back and cream spots. Freshwater specimens generally are dark green or brown above with numerous red or orange dots on the sides. Some have wormlike markings. One sure way to distinguish it from the Arctic Char is to count the gill rakers. The Dolly Varden has a maximum of 21 while the Char has 23-32.

SIZE: Like its coloration, its size varies widely with habitat. In Alaskan streams, many over 5 pounds are taken, but that would be unusual in the Lower States, except in large lakes. World record 19 pounds, 4 ounces.

FOOD VALUE: Early sea-run fish are excellent; freshwater specimens quite good, especially when smoked.

GAME QUALITIES: Although many anglers in the past regarded the Dolly as not much more than a trash fish and a depredator of Salmon, they are now getting their due recognition as a terrific gamefish that fights with great strength, if not very acrobatically.

TACKLE: Spinning, baitcasting and fly tackle all are used with effect.

LURES AND BAITS: Adult fish will feed on insects at times but are mostly fish-eaters and best lured by streamer flies, spoons, spinners, plugs and live bait. Best natural baits are Salmon eggs and minnows.

RANGE: *Pacific Coast watersheds, Alaska to Oregon.*

WHERE TO FISH: *Along beaches near river mouths, and in many streams, large and small. Also inhabits lakes, and some populations are landlocked.*

Bull Trout

Salvelinus confluentus

OTHER NAMES:

Western Brook Trout
Rocky Mountain Trout
Red Spotted Char

RANGE: *Most common in British Columbia, Manitoba, Washington, Idaho and western Montana. Also found in Oregon, northern California and northern Nevada.*

WHERE TO FISH: *Deep pools of very cold rivers and large lakes at high elevations.*

DESCRIPTION: So similar to the Dolly Varden that many anglers and a few scientists do not distinguish them. The Bull Trout's head is longer and flatter than the Dolly's and the eye is located higher on the head.

SIZE: Reaches at least 3 feet and 30 pounds, but catches commonly run about 1 to 5 pounds. World record 32 pounds.

FOOD VALUE: Very good.

GAME QUALITIES: Stubborn fighter but not showy.

TACKLE: Since deep fishing produces most Bull Trout, baitcasting and stout spinning gear are the best choices. Fly fishing can produce some action in August and September but, again, flies must be fished deep.

LURES AND BAITS: Live baitfish, cut baits, spoons, diving plugs, weighted streamers and wet flies.

Atlantic Salmon

Salmo salar

DESCRIPTION: Early sea-run fish are bright silver with steel-blue back and tiny black spots, most of them above the lateral line. The spots are generally shaped like tiny crosses. Adult fish running to fresh water for the first time are called grilse, and have forked tails. Tails of larger adults on succeeding runs are square. Color and condition gradually deteriorate while fish are in the rivers until, after spawning, they get very thin and dark and are often called "black salmon," although a more widely accepted term for post-spawn salmon is "kelt."

SIZE: Grilse average about 2 to 8 pounds. Size of adults varies considerably by the waters fished. Some large rivers are famous for Salmon weighing upwards of 30 pounds and potentially to 50 or more, while other, smaller streams seldom see a fish topping 15 pounds. World record 79 pounds, 2 ounces (from Norway).

FOOD VALUE: Ranks among the best.

GAME QUALITIES: Early-run fish have speed, strength, great stamina and spectacular leaping ability. Few gamefish are their equal.

TACKLE: In North America, much fishing is done with fly tackle, which is required in some waters. No. 8 and 9 outfits are ideal, but No. 10 or 11 rigs are sometimes needed to reach big Salmon with big flies in big water. Conditions permitting, veterans often choose much lighter outfits, particularly for dry-fly fishing in smaller streams or during low-water periods.

LURES AND BAITS: Wet flies are the most productive everywhere, with each locality having its own preference in pattern. In low water, big dry flies work very well.

OTHER NAMES:

Kennebec Salmon
Black Salmon
Kelt

RANGE: *Atlantic Provinces of Canada and a few streams in Maine. Introduced to the Great Lakes.*

WHERE TO FISH: *Atlantic Salmon are anadromous, spawning in clear, cold streams. They vigorously pursue their upstream spawning travels but rest in pools and deep runs, where most fishing takes place.*

Landlocked Salmon

Salmo salar

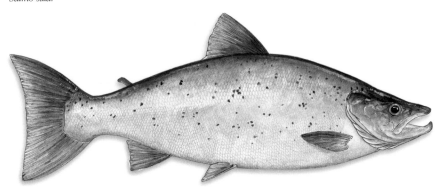

OTHER NAMES:

Sebago Salmon
Ouananiche

RANGE: *Canada's Maritime Provinces, New England and New York. Maine is the center of its popularity.*

WHERE TO FISH: *Its early life is spent in rivers tributary to large lakes, but most fishing is done in river mouths and open lakes.*

DESCRIPTION: Scientifically, this fish is no different from the Atlantic Salmon, but to anglers, nearly everything about it is different, starting with appearance. Although color can vary in different lakes, the Landlocked is proportionally longer and usually much darker than the anadromous Atlantic Salmon and its spots are more liberally sprinkled over the entire sides. Background color ranges from tan or olive to dark gray.

SIZE: Averages 2-5 pounds. Fish over 10 pounds are rare. World record 19 pounds, 4 ounces.

FOOD VALUE: Excellent.

GAME QUALITIES: Has everything the anadromous Atlantic Salmon does, except size.

TACKLE: Fly tackle is used successfully for casting in the lower stretches of rivers and for drifting or trolling in the lakes. Spinning and baitcasting tackle are excellent producers with either lures or live bait. Long limber trolling rods are used in larger lakes.

LURES AND BAITS: Adult Landlocks feed primarily on small forage fishes, so preferred lures are streamer flies and spoons.

Brown Trout
Salmo trutta

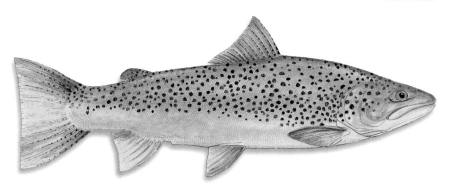

DESCRIPTION: Browns in rivers and creeks are among the most colorful of Trouts, tan to brown or pale yellow on the sides and plentifully sprinkled with black, brown and red spots on sides and gill covers. Sea-run fish are silvery with cross-shaped spots on upper sides.

SIZE: Although the world record is 40 pounds and fish over 20 pounds are sometimes taken in the Great Lakes and other large lakes and rivers, the average size in most streams of North America is 1 or 2 pounds, often smaller, and a fish of 4 pounds or more is always a prize. World record 40 pounds, 4 ounces.

FOOD VALUE: Small ones are excellent and big ones darn good.

GAME QUALITIES: Considered the toughest of Trout to fool with flies. They are also strong and determined fighters that can uncork some wild jumps.

TACKLE: Most fly rodders consider the Brown the No. 1 challenge. Lightweight rods are the norm on small streams. Heavier fly tackle and spinning rods get the call on big rivers or for deep-trolling in lakes.

LURES AND BAITS: Big flies such as streamers and muddlers draw heavy duty in most streams, since large Browns are omnivorous, shoveling in aquatic and terrestrial insects, crawfish and baitfish without much preference. In small steams, dry flies often produce well, but only when most carefully presented. Various nymphs and terrestrials may be the most productive lures. Tiny spinning lures and a variety of natural baits are used with effect. For big-water trolling, diving plugs and spoons are productive, and downriggers are often needed.

OTHER NAMES:

European Brown
German Brown
Brownie

RANGE: Introduced to North America from Europe in the 19th century, the Brown has since been introduced to every state where Trout are fished, and also stocked widely in Canada.

WHERE TO FISH: Browns feed primarily in quiet pools and smooth runs. They like areas where there are obstacles or undercut banks. Biggest fish are found in major lakes and large rivers, especially tailwaters of dams. In the Great Lakes and other big waters, deep trolling accounts for a lot of good-sized Brownies.

Rainbow Trout

Oncorhynchus mykiss

OTHER NAMES:

Steelhead
Kamloops

RANGE: *Native to the Pacific slopes of North America from Alaska to northern Mexico, the Rainbow is the most widely transplanted of all Trout and is now familiar in all states where Trout are fished, including Hawaii, as well as in much of Canada.*

WHERE TO FISH: *Handles warmer temperatures than most other Trout. Feeds most actively in riffles and other fast water, but is at home in lakes and quiet pools. Again, bigger waters hold bigger fish.*

DESCRIPTION: As with other Trout, color can vary from one body of water to the next. In clear lakes, fish may be almost colorless but most mature Rainbows (except the Steelhead; see next entry) do have a characteristic broad, red slash from head to tail. The body is gray-blue or olive above the lateral line, silvery below. Sides, dorsal fin and tail are dotted.

SIZE: A good rule of thumb is: the bigger the water the bigger the Rainbows. In small streams they average less than a pound, but 2- to 4-pounders are common in larger rivers and many lakes, and specimens exceeding 5 pounds are not rare. In fact, Rainbows over 20 pounds are taken in big water, such as Lake Pend Oreille in Utah, where fish over 30 pounds are always possible. Similar huge fish also roam some big waters in western Canada and Alaska. World record 42 pounds, 2 ounces (Steelhead); 37 pounds for inland form.

FOOD VALUE: Varies from good (hatchery or commercial fish) to excellent.

GAME QUALITIES: A favorite of fishermen and with good reason. Rainbows combine exceptional strength with a flair for showy jumping.

TACKLE: Anything goes, from fly tackle to cane poles, and even heavy spinning or baitcasting gear when trolling in large lakes. A lot depends on the angler's attitude, plus the particular waters fished.

LURES AND BAITS: Not particularly elusive, but no dummy either, Rainbows on most waters take dry and sinking flies, streamers, small spinners, small spoons, trolling plugs and too many natural baits to count, including canned corn and marshmallows, in addition to the usual worms, grasshoppers, salmon eggs, small fish and other natural forage.

Steelhead

Oncorhynchus mykiss

DESCRIPTION: The Steelhead is the migratory or anadromous version of the Rainbow Trout. It enters rivers as a bright silvery fish with steel-blue back and small black dots on the upper sides, dorsal fin and tail—beautiful but not as colorful as it is likely to become after extended time in fresh water, when its color gradually darkens and eventually may develop the characteristic red slash of most other Rainbows.

SIZE: Averages 10 or 15 pounds, with some fish running 20 to 30. World record 42 pounds, 2 ounces.

FOOD VALUE: Excellent.

GAME QUALITIES: Tops. Fly fishermen compare the Steelhead to Atlantic Salmon in fighting ability, and with good reason.

TACKLE: A premier fly fish, the Steelhead usually is challenged with fairly heavy fly equipment—No. 8 or 9. Because of clear water, long casts are essential and most regulars use shooting heads to achieve greater distances than even a weight-forward line can provide. The best spinning outfits for Steelhead fishing feature long, supple rods.

LURES AND BAITS: Not surprisingly, favorite flies vary from river to river, but a great many are effective—all fast-sinking types. Bright colors, such as pink, orange and yellow, mark many productive patterns. Spin fishermen use a variety of spinners and spoons, many of which blend the flash of metal with reds or other brilliant hues. Salmon eggs rate as the top natural bait.

OTHER NAMES:

**Rainbow Trout
Steelie
Chromer**

RANGE: On the Pacific Coast, prime steelhead fishing extends from northern California to Alaska. Steelhead runs also occur in tributary streams of the Great Lakes and, to a much smaller extent, the North Atlantic.

WHERE TO FISH: Like migrating Salmon, Steelhead will struggle against rapids and rushing water to reach their spawning grounds, but are usually fished in deep pools or behind rocks where the flow is pronounced but moderate. Also like Salmon, they tend to favor the same "lies," and so relying on local knowledge is the best way to find them.

Cutthroat Trout

Oncorhynchus clarki

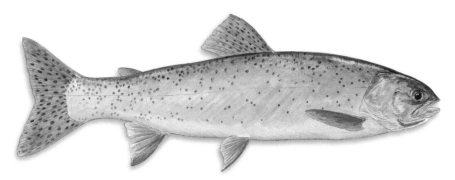

OTHER NAMES:

Black-spotted Trout
Red-throated Trout
many local names

OTHER NAMES:

Black-spotted Trout
Red-throated Trout
many local names

RANGE: *Considered the "native" western Trout (although Rainbows also are native), Cutthroats occur in anadromous populations in many streams from northern California to Prince William Sound, Alaska. Inland populations cover most of the mountainous areas from Alberta south to New Mexico.*

WHERE TO FISH: *Inhabits lakes and rivers and in some areas, particularly British Columbia, is often fished in estuaries. Inland fishing generally is more productive in small streams and tributaries than in large rivers.*

DESCRIPTION: The Cutthroat gets its name from red lines on either side of the lower jaw. This and a profusion of black dots on the sides, tail and dorsal fin are about the only consistent identifying features, because coloration is widely variable in different areas, and confused even more by the fact that Cutthroats readily hybridize with other Trout species in many waters. There are four major subspecies of Cutthroat and more less common subspecies having an array of color patterns.

SIZE: The average in most small streams is a pound or less. Fish up to 6 pounds or so may come from lakes and larger rivers, and even bigger ones from deep lakes and salt water. Although a 41-pounder is the world record, 10- to 15-pounders are unusual today.

FOOD VALUE: Excellent.

GAME QUALITIES: A fine gamefish, although generally not as acrobatic as the Rainbow.

TACKLE: Fly fishermen mostly work the small streams and lean toward lighter outfits, around No. 5, on average. Spinning tackle ranges from ultralight in creeks and ponds to medium-heavy for casting and trolling in some big lakes.

LURES AND BAITS: Cutthroats are often good, but wary, targets for dry flies. Of course, wet flies, nymphs and small streamers are very productive. Good natural baits include minnows and worms. Flashy spinners and spoons are the leading hard lures—using tiny models in small streams and moving up in lure size as the water depth increases.

Golden Trout
Oncorhynchus aguabonita

DESCRIPTION: The pure strain is the prettiest of all the Trout. Its back is olive green, shading to gold on the sides, with yellowish belly. A series of dark olive oval or round spots runs along the side from gill to tail beneath a full-length red stripe. Smaller spots are on the tail and upper body.

SIZE: Usually less than a pound, but can reach several pounds in lakes. World record 11 pounds.

FOOD VALUE: Excellent.

GAME QUALITIES: A spirited fighter.

TACKLE: The lightest fly and ultralight spinning gear.

LURES AND BAITS: Tiny flies are best, about Nos. 12-18. Dries often work but nymphs are more dependable. Spin fishermen mostly use either flies with bubbles or else very tiny in-line spinners.

OTHER NAMES:

Volcano Creek Trout
Kern River Trout

RANGE: *Originally found in Volcano Creek off Kern River in the high Sierras of California, it has been transplanted to other creeks, rivers and lakes in the high country of California and some other western states.*

WHERE TO FISH: *The pure strain thrives only at elevations of about 6,000 feet or more, but Goldens hybridize readily with both Cutthroat and Rainbow Trout, and the hybrids can be encountered at lower elevations.*

Chinook Salmon

Oncorhynchus tshawytscha

OTHER NAMES:

King Salmon
Tyee
Quinnat
Blackmouth

RANGE: The Pacific Coast from northern California to Alaska. They have been introduced into all the Great Lakes, as well as to other lakes in several states, but do not reproduce in any of those areas and so fishable populations are dependent on regular restocking.

WHERE TO FISH: Pacific anglers concentrate their efforts mostly in bays and estuaries where the fish gather for their spawning runs from late spring to early fall. They are also heavily fished in the lower reaches of the spawning rivers themselves. Smaller numbers are taken far upstream. In the Great Lakes, offshore trolling is popular in summer.

DESCRIPTION: In the sea or the Great Lakes, the Chinook is basically silver in color, shading to blue or blue-green on the upper sides and darker blue on the back. It is profusely spotted above the lateral line, on the dorsal and tail. Breeding fish are darker in color, often green or purplish. Kings are distinguishable from other Salmons of similar size by the gums at the base of the teeth, which are black.

SIZE: Largest of the Salmons, adult Chinook weighing 10-20 pounds are commonly caught, while 40- and 50-pounders are not unusual. World record 97 pounds, 4 ounces.

FOOD VALUE: Excellent fresh or smoked.

GAME QUALITIES: Strength and size make Kings formidable fighters. They seldom break the surface but have a lot of stamina and plenty of underwater tricks to play.

TACKLE: In the Pacific and the Great Lakes, stout spinning outfits, baitcasting rigs and light saltwater tackle all have their devotees. Another standard western outfit is a long fly rod fitted with a large, single-action reel. Any and all of that gear is used for trolling with downriggers or heavy weights, and also for still fishing with sinkers and natural bait. Deep jigging with stout spinning and baitcasting gear is effective in some coastal areas. Spinning and casting gear, along with heavy fly tackle, get the nod for stream fishing.

LURES AND BAITS: Most Kings are taken either on deep-trolled lures such as large spoons and diving plugs, or on live and cut bait. Bright dodgers or flashers rigged ahead of the lures add greatly to the number of strikes. Casters in the rivers rely mostly on spoons and spinners. Fly rodders lean to streamer flies, usually with sinking lines.

Coho Salmon
Oncorhynchus kisutch

DESCRIPTION: Steel-blue back with silvery sides and white belly. Usually less spotted than the King Salmon, and only the lower lobe of the caudal fin is spotted. It is further distinguishable by the gums, which are white. Breeding fish in the rivers grow darker in color, with olive back and red sides.

SIZE: Usually weighs in the range of 2 to 6 pounds, but 10-pound fish are fairly common along much of the West Coast and in Lake Michigan. Tops is around 20 pounds. World record 33 pounds, 4 ounces.

FOOD VALUE: Excellent fresh or smoked.

GAME QUALITIES: Fights with speed and strength. Also jumps frequently, especially when hooked near the surface.

TACKLE: For deep trolling in estuaries or big lakes, heavy spinning gear is popular, with large level-wind reels and, in the Pacific, single-action reels with long rods. At times—more so in the Pacific than the Great Lakes—Cohos school and feed at the surface, making exciting casting targets with light spinning and fly tackle. The same kinds of light tackle are used in river fishing.

LURES AND BAITS: A great deal of fishing is done with large spoons, plugs and whole baitfish or rigged fillets. Trolling probably heads the list of approaches, although drifting with live or cut baitfish is close. Live forage in the Pacific includes Herring, Candlefish and Sardines. In the Great Lakes, Cohos gorge mainly on Alewives and Smelt. Metallic lures and shiny streamer flies are the ticket for spin and fly casting.

OTHER NAMES:

Silver Salmon
Blueback

RANGE: *Natural range is on the Pacific Coast from northern California to Alaska. Transplanted to all the Great Lakes and a few other lakes, it is reproducing only in Lakes Michigan and Superior but, even there, natural reproduction is insufficient to maintain a viable angling population. Good stocking programs keep fishermen happy.*

WHERE TO FISH: *Although wide-open water along the Pacific Coast and in the Great Lakes is the busiest angling scene, much fishing is done in rivers as well. Cohos do not feed while on their spawning runs upstream but, like Atlantic Salmon, can be induced to strike nonetheless.*

Sockeye Salmon

Oncorhynchus nerka

OTHER NAMES:

Red Salmon
Blueback Salmon
Kokanee Salmon

RANGE: *From the Sacramento River drainage in California to arctic Alaska, but not common south of the Columbia River (Oregon-Washington).*

WHERE TO FISH: *Widely fished from the estuaries to far upriver during spawning runs.*

DESCRIPTION: In salt water, the Sockeye has bright silvery sides with bluish back and tiny black dots on the back and tail fin. During upstream runs the color changes dramatically to the "Red Salmon" phase. The male has a bright red body and green head. The female's colors are similar but duller.

SIZE: Most catches run from 4-8 pounds or so. Maximum is probably 14 or 15. World record 15 pounds, 3 ounces.

FOOD VALUE: Considered the best of the Salmons, whether fresh, smoked or canned. The flesh is red and rich.

GAME QUALITIES: Great fighters, despite lagging behind the Chinook and Coho in publicity and angling prestige.

TACKLE: Heavy spinning and light baitcasting tackle for estuaries and big water. Upriver, fly tackle can be productive, but the fish do not rise well, and so sinking lines are called for in deep water.

LURES AND BAITS: Large flies are often used in estuaries and lower reaches of rivers, but are more often trolled or drifted than cast. Along with spoons and other flashy metallic lures, the flies are fished deep (using sinkers) with spinning or baitcasting gear. Fly casting is practical and popular in many upstream areas, and very bright flies always seem to work best.

The Whitefishes

8

Inconnu

Stenodus leucichthys

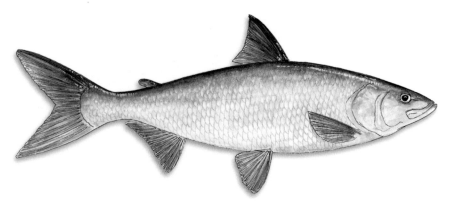

OTHER NAMES:

Sheefish
Conny or Connie
Eskimo Tarpon

RANGE: *Arctic drainages of Alaska and northwestern Canada.*

WHERE TO FISH: *Sheefish are migratory, but only in fresh water; they do not run to sea. Best fishing is in rivers during spawning runs in summer, but many lakes hold Sheefish as well. Not many sportfishermen ever get—or seek—the chance to go after them.*

DESCRIPTION: Because of its silvery color and large scooped mouth, the Sheefish has been referred to as the "Tarpon of the Arctic." The back is blue or brown, sides silver, underside white. Scales are large and the tail is forked. The jaw extends past the eye.

SIZE: Fish weighing 10-20 pounds are common and much larger ones are always possible. Maximum is 50 or more. World record 53 pounds.

FOOD VALUE: Good.

GAME QUALITIES: Most of those hooked are good-size fish, strong, deep-running and determined.

TACKLE: Spinning is the best bet. Fly fishing sometimes pays off.

LURES AND BAITS: Spoons and spinners; streamer flies.

Arctic Grayling
Thymallus arcticus

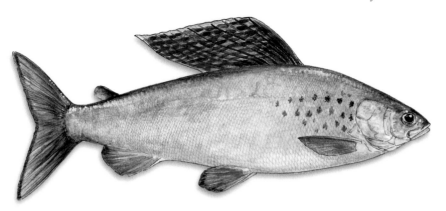

DESCRIPTION: Easily identified by the sail-like dorsal fin, which is purple or black and marked with rows of vivid spots. Colors are variable with location, but it is usually dark with an overall metallic cast, either silvery or brassy. The mouth is very small.

SIZE: A 2-pound grayling is a prize in any water. Occasionally reaches 4 or 5 pounds. World record 5 pounds, 15 ounces.

FOOD VALUE: Excellent.

GAME QUALITIES: Spirited and active fighter on light tackle.

TACKLE: Fly fishing with light gear, No. 5 or even smaller, reigns supreme for Grayling, but ultralight spinning gets action as well.

LURES AND BAITS: Grayling are wary but respond well to small dry flies fished on very thin leaders. Tiny spinners and spoons do the job for spin fishermen.

OTHER NAMES:

Grayling
American Grayling
Montana Grayling

RANGE: *Common from west of Hudson Bay across northwest Canada to Alaska and south to Central Alberta. Small population in upper Missouri River drainage of Montana. Introduced elsewhere.*

WHERE TO FISH: *In rivers, Grayling lurk in protected pockets behind rocks. In lakes, they often are found along rocky shorelines. Grayling run in schools and inhabit clear water, so they frequently can be located by sight.*

Mountain Whitefish

Prosopium williamsoni

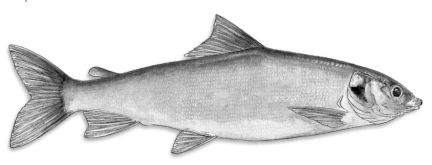

OTHER NAMES:

Rocky Mountain Whitefish

Williamson's Whitefish

RANGE: *Inhabits both streams and lakes of northwestern states and western Canadian provinces, chiefly British Columbia.*

WHERE TO FISH: *Mountain Whitefish basically like the same sort of water as trout, feeding on insects and larvae in the fast water of streams, and deep water of lakes. Lake fish also work ledges and rocks along shorelines.*

DESCRIPTION: A silvery fish with brown or olive back. The dorsal fin is high and dusky.

SIZE: Averages a pound or so. Frequently tops 2 pounds and may reach 5. World record 5 pounds, 8 ounces.

FOOD VALUE: Very good.

GAME QUALITIES: Although belittled by trout fishermen, Mountain Whitefish are nevertheless good fighters that often provide action when the more glamorous types are reluctant to hit.

TACKLE: Fly fishing produces lots of action, but anglers seeking Whitefish specifically are more likely to choose light spinning tackle.

LURES AND BAITS: Best flies are nymphs, although dries sometimes turn them on. Salmon eggs make the best bait, but worms are good too.

Round Whitefish

Prosopium cylindraceum

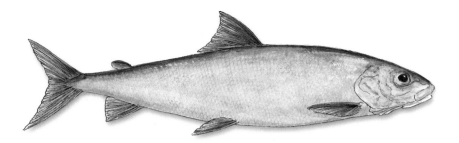

DESCRIPTION: Color is similar to the Mountain Whitefish, but the shape is more cylindrical and the snout slightly more pointed. Confusion of the two species is seldom a problem, however, as their ranges do not overlap.

SIZE: Usually a pound or less. Maximum is around 5 pounds. World record 6 pounds.

FOOD VALUE: Very good.

GAME QUALITIES: Scrappy fighter on light gear.

TACKLE: Fly or spinning in streams and lake margins. Spinning in deeper waters of lakes.

LURES AND BAITS: Susceptible in streams to nymphs and other sinking flies. In lakes, small spinners are best, especially if tipped with a maggot, salmon egg or other natural bait.

OTHER NAMES:

**Menominee
Round Fish
Frost Fish
Pilot Fish**

RANGE: *From Ontario and Lake Superior eastward through the border states and New England, widespread in northern Canada and Alaska.*

WHERE TO FISH: *Inhabits many streams and lakes of northern Canada, but most fish in the southern part of the range are found in deep lakes.*

Lake Whitefish

Coregonus clupeaformis

OTHER NAMES:

**High Back
Common
 Whitefish
Eastern Whitefish
Inland Whitefish
Gizzard Fish**

RANGE: *Border states northward through most of Canada and Alaska.*

WHERE TO FISH: *In the Great Lakes and other more southerly waters of its range, the Lake Whitefish stays deep and is not a prominent sporting catch. Farther north, it frequents shallower waters of both streams and lakes and so becomes a better angling target.*

DESCRIPTION: Deep-bodied with narrow head and small mouth. Overall bright silver color with brownish back.

SIZE: Averages about 1 pound; commonly reaches 4 pounds or so, and occasionally hits 10 pounds or a little more. World record 14 pounds, 6 ounces.

FOOD VALUE: Excellent.

GAME QUALITIES: Frisky fighter on light tackle as it runs well, rolls at the surface and even gets off an occasional jump.

TACKLE: Spinning tackle is productive in both lakes and rivers. Fly fishing often good in streams.

LURES AND BAITS: Small spinners and spoons serve the spin fisherman well. Dry flies pay off during hatches. In deep water, best natural baits are minnows and cut pieces of fish. Crappie tackle can double for whitefish.

Cisco

Coregonus artedi

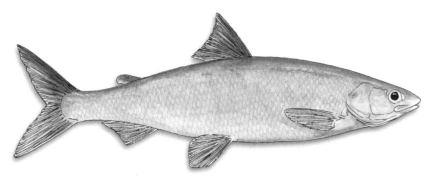

DESCRIPTION: There are several quite similar species of Cisco in various northern waters but this is the one of chief interest to sportfishermen. It is elongated and cylindrical in shape, with blue back and silver sides. The mouth is very small.

SIZE: Most weigh about a pound, but 2- to 3-pounders are fairly common in some lakes and the potential is to 6 or 7 pounds. World record 7 pounds, 6 ounces.

FOOD VALUE: Very good, especially smoked or canned.

GAME QUALITIES: Spunky fighter for its size on light line or tippet.

TACKLE: Light fly tackle, No. 5 or less, provides most sport. Ultralight spinning can be used with effect, as can ice-fishing rigs.

LURES AND BAITS: Dry flies; tiny jigs, spoons and spinners. Small minnows make the best natural bait.

OTHER NAMES:

Lake Herring
Chub
Nipigon
Tulibee

RANGE: In the United States, from the upper Mississippi basin and Great Lakes eastward to the Adirondacks and New England. Widespread in Canada.

WHERE TO FISH: Lakes and large rivers. Cisco stay deep most of the time but provide great fun when they romp near the surface—usually during late evening in spring and summer. Many are also caught under the ice in winter.

For fun, food and availability it would be difficult to top the Catfish family. Its smaller members—familiarly known as Bullheads—abound in nearly ever pond, creek, ditch or canal in the land, and can readily be caught on improvised tackle and all sorts of easy-to-get baits. Larger species of Catfish roam most of our bigger waterways—rivers, lakes, impoundments. Their size makes them fine gamefish but, even so, they are just as tasty as the little Bullheads and are often just as easy to please when it comes to bait selection; however, live baitfish are a top choice if you hope to bag a real lunker. The biggest North American members of this family are the Blue and Flathead Catfish, both of which often push 50 pounds in weight and sometimes exceed 100. The Channel Cat is a middleweight, topping out at about 50 pounds but far more often running well under 10. In fact, small Channel Cats are highly valued by fishermen because they have a reputation as the best table variety. It's doubtful though, that you could taste any difference in a mixed platter of fried Catfish from the same waters. In addition to being fine sportfish on rod or pole, Catfish also provide a great deal of pleasure to thousands of people who go after them with other kinds of gear, primarily trotlines, bush lines, and lines rigged below floating plastic jugs.

The Catfishes

Black Bullhead

Ameiurus melas

OTHER NAMES:

Mudcat

Horned Pout

RANGE: *Most of the U.S. heartland from the Appalachians to The Plains. Extends southward to the Gulf States (except Florida), and northward into southern Ontario and Manitoba.*

WHERE TO FISH: *Hugs the bottom in still or slowly moving waters. Night fishing is most productive.*

DESCRIPTION: Back is dusky and sides dingy or sooty. No mottling on sides. Anal fin is rounded and tail is square. Chin barbels are dark gray or black.

SIZE: Basically the same as the Brown and Yellow Bullheads, but may grow a bit larger. World record 7 pounds, 7 ounces.

FOOD VALUE: Very good.

GAME QUALITIES: Spunky but a lightweight.

TACKLE: Pole, light spinning.

LURES AND BAITS: Any of the popular small natural baits, plus cheese, corn, or doughballs. Nightcrawlers are an all-time favorite.

Blue Catfish

Ictalurus furcatus

DESCRIPTION: Very similar to the Channel Cat, but not spotted. Quickest point of identification is the anal fin, which is long and straight in the Blue Cat; rounded in the Channel.

SIZE: Largest of the Catfish, it often exceeds 50 pounds and can reach at least 100 pounds. Many catches are hefty, running perhaps 20 or 30 pounds. World record 116 pounds, 12 ounces.

FOOD VALUE: Very good.

GAME QUALITIES: Size and strength make them rugged foes for the angler.

TACKLE: Rather heavy baitcasting, spinning and even light saltwater gear. Also trotlines and "jug lines," which are lines suspended from free-floating plastic jugs.

LURES AND BAITS: Live baits are fine—fish and crawfish in particular—although large cut baits or chunks of meat will work. Dip and prepared baits are effective in still water.

OTHER NAMES:

Silver Catfish
Bagre Azul

RANGE: Native to the Mississippi River and Rio Grande drainages and some lesser Gulf of Mexico drainages. Introduced to many rivers along the Atlantic Coast.

WHERE TO FISH: Blue Cats favor flowing rivers with reasonably clean water and hard bottom. Try deep holes and dropoffs, or drift deep baits downstream, in the current.

Brown Bullhead

Ameiurus nebulosus

OTHER NAMES:

Squaretail Catfish
Common Pout
Brown Catfish

RANGE: *Most of eastern North America from Florida to New Brunswick and Nova Scotia. Extends westward to the Dakotas and southern Manitoba. Widely transplanted elsewhere.*

WHERE TO FISH: *Ponds, lakes and slow streams. Feeds on or near bottom. Night fishing is most productive.*

DESCRIPTION: Color is brown above, with cream or yellow sides with brown mottling. The tail is nearly square.

SIZE: Most are under a pound. Commonly reaches 2 pounds and can grow to 5 or so. World record 6 pounds, 1 ounce.

FOOD VALUE: Very good.

GAME QUALITIES: Cooperative and fun to catch on light gear.

TACKLE: Pole, spinning tackle.

LURES AND BAITS: Worms and other small natural baits. Cheese, bread and liver are also good.

Channel Catfish

Ictalurus punctatus

DESCRIPTION: Light blue or gray on top, silvery below, with many black spots sprinkled over the sides of smaller specimens. Large fish lose the spots and are often almost black. The anal fin is rounded.

SIZE: Common from 6 inches to about 4 pounds, but much bigger fish are not unusual. The potential is to more than 50 pounds. World record 58 pounds.

FOOD VALUE: Excellent.

GAME QUALITIES: Fish of decent size resist strongly and with stamina.

TACKLE: Poles or light spinning for small fish; heavier spinning and baitcasting for bigger ones. Also trotlines and bush lines, where legal.

LURES AND BAITS: Anything from live baitfish and crawfish to cut bait, liver and homemade concoctions. Anglers after panfish take many Channel Cats on such baits as crickets, grubs and worms. Channel Cats also will strike many different lures, but artificial baits are not chosen by those who fish for them deliberately.

OTHER NAMES:

**Speckled Cat
River Cat**

RANGE: *Native to most of the U.S. east of the Rockies, and to border areas of Canada, but now found just about every- where, including Hawaii, thanks to stocking.*

WHERE TO FISH: *Flowing streams provide the best fishing for Channel Cats but many lakes hold them as well. Fish deep holes during the day. In lakes try areas close to where streams flow in.*

Flathead Catfish

Pylodictis olivaris

OTHER NAMES:

Mudcat

Shovelhead Catfish

Apaloosa Cat

Yellow Cat

RANGE: *About the same as that of the Blue Catfish, but more widely transplanted to other areas as far west as California.*

WHERE TO FISH: *Large rivers and reservoirs. Less active than the Blue and Channel Cats, Flatheads are often caught in flowing current but also like calmer spots, such as eddies and backwaters. Nightfishing is best for larger flatheads.*

DESCRIPTION: The head is wide and flat and the tail square. Color is brown overall with shadings of yellow or gold. The tip of the upper lobe of the tail is white.

SIZE: Another very large catfish, the Flathead is common at 15-35 pounds and sometimes exceeds 50, although most catches probably are in the 8- to 15-pound range. Maximum potential is around 100 pounds. World record 123 pounds, 9 ounces.

FOOD VALUE: Excellent.

GAME QUALITIES: A tough but not spectacular fighter.

TACKLE: Many small fish are caught on poles and light spinning or casting gear, but the big boys require heavy lines and stouter rods. Trotlines and jug lines are also used.

LURES AND BAITS: Live fish are best for Flatheads of trophy size. Smaller ones will take the full range of Catfish and panfish baits, including earthworms and cut baits of both aquatic and kitchen origins.

Snail Bullhead

Ameiurus brunneus

DESCRIPTION: Color is olive above, yellowish on sides. Some are mottled while others are plain. Large dark spot at base of dorsal fin. Tail is square and tipped in black.

SIZE: Very small; to not much more than half a pound.

FOOD VALUE: Excellent.

GAME QUALITIES: Spunky but a lightweight.

TACKLE: Pole, light spinning.

LURES AND BAITS: All the popular small natural baits, plus corn, cheese and doughballs.

OTHER NAMES:

Mudcat
Speckled Cat

RANGE: *The Carolinas, Georgia and North Florida.*

WHERE TO FISH: *Prefers faster water than other Bullheads. Try feeder creeks and small rivers.*

Spotted Bullhead

Ameiurus serracanthus

OTHER NAMES:

Speckled Cat

RANGE: *Restricted areas in the Florida Panhandle, southern Georgia and southern Alabama.*

WHERE TO FISH: *Ponds, shallow reservoirs and slow streams.*

DESCRIPTION: Dark brown above and tan on the sides, with numerous white spots. The tail is square and the fins are rimmed in black.

SIZE: Usually 8-12 inches long; seldom exceeds 2 pounds in weight.

FOOD VALUE: Excellent.

GAME QUALITIES: Not big enough to pull hard.

TACKLE: Poles are best but spinning gear is good too.

LURES AND BAITS: Worms, cheese, doughballs, small minnows and other natural offerings.

Stonecat
Noturus flavus

DESCRIPTION: Wide head and slender body. The tail is rounded and has a white streak on the rear upward edge. Overall color varies from gray to light yellow.

SIZE: Usually a few ounces; possibly approaches 1 pound on rare occasions.

FOOD VALUE: Fair.

GAME QUALITIES: Poor.

TACKLE: Pole.

LURES AND BAITS: Grubs and bits of earthworm; also cheese and doughballs.

RANGE: *The upper half of the U.S., from Montana and Wyoming eastward to New England.*

WHERE TO FISH: *Likes rocky bottom in flowing water, but also is found in hard-bottomed lakes.*

Walking Catfish

Clarias batrachus

RANGE: *Common in South Florida. Sometimes found in other parts of Florida, or even in other states, where it is sometimes introduced from private collections.*

WHERE TO FISH: *Usually caught in Florida from Lake Okeechobee southward.*

DESCRIPTION: An aquarium introduction from Asia, it only superficially resembles native Catfish species. The body is long, thin and dark gray, with rounded tail. The mouth is flat and has eight barbels. The pectoral fins curve downward and serve as "legs" when the fish travels on land, which it can do because portions of its gills have been modified to permit breathing of air.

SIZE: Most are 10 or 12 inches long. Some weigh as much as a pound. World record 1 pound, 8 ounces.

FOOD VALUE: Poor; too scrawny.

GAME QUALITIES: Poor.

TACKLE: Light spinning.

LURES AND BAITS: Sometimes takes a worm or other panfish bait. Night fishing is most productive.

White Catfish

Ameiurus catus

DESCRIPTION: Back and sides are varying shades of gray and blue. Underparts are white. The tail is slightly forked, with rounded lobes.

SIZE: Usually a pound or so, but fairly common to about 3 pounds. Few exceed that weight, although fish larger than 15 pounds are on record. World record 18 pounds, 4 ounces.

FOOD VALUE: Excellent.

GAME QUALITIES: A good fighter, but a lightweight.

TACKLE: Pole, light spinning, light baitcasting.

LURES AND BAITS: Best are earthworms, crickets, grubs and cut baits. Like most Catfish, the White will gobble just about anything organic. Also takes flies and small lures at times.

OTHER NAMES:

Potomac Catfish

RANGE: *Coastal streams from the Mid-Atlantic States to Louisiana. Introduced to many other waters, including lakes and ponds in the Northeast and other parts of the country.*

WHERE TO FISH: *Prefers slow-moving areas of streams or weed edges in lakes.*

Yellow Bullhead

Ameiurus natalis

DESCRIPTION: Brown on top, yellowish below. The tail is square and the chin barbels are white.

SIZE: Usually less than a pound; occasionally 2 pounds or more. World record 4 pounds, 4 ounces.

FOOD VALUE: Very good.

GAME QUALITIES: Fun to catch but no great challenge.

TACKLE: Pole, light and ultralight spinning.

LURES AND BAITS: Any of the popular small natural baits, plus cheese, corn, or doughballs.

OTHER NAMES:

Butterball
Butter Cat
Polliwog

RANGE: *Most of the U.S. from the Plains States to the Atlantic Coast. Also found in southeastern Canada, and has been widely transplanted.*

WHERE TO FISH: *Likes still water and feeds on bottom. Good fish for stocked ponds.*

Most experienced anglers are well aware that certain species of fish live most of their lives at sea but must ascend freshwater streams to spawn. Striped Bass, Shad and many members of the Salmon family are examples of such fish, which are labeled "anadromous." But in addition to the anadromous types, many of our freshwater rivers contain fish that are, without question, saltwater species. Generally speaking, they go upriver to seek more suitable temperatures or better feeding grounds, and later return to salt water. It's not at all unusual, however, for some of those saltwater fish to like their sweetwater environs so much that they don't bother to leave. Others become landlocked in one way or another and easily adapt to their new homes although, in most cases, they cannot spawn. Along the Atlantic and Gulf coasts, Snook, Striped Bass, Tarpon, Red Drum and Spotted Seatrout are familiar freshwater targets, especially during cold weather. On the Pacific Coast, the Orangemouth Corvina and other saltwater fish have turned out to be just the ticket for anglers in a huge salt California lake called the Salton Sea. Corvina and some other saltwater fish are also found in the Colorado River, having entered from the Sea of Cortez.

Saltwater Refugees

Atlantic Needlefish

Atlantic Stingray

Atlantic Tomcod

Bairdiella

Bull Shark

Common Snook

Fat Snook

Gray Snapper

Ladyfish

Orangemouth Corvina

Red Drum

Sargo

Sheepshead

Silver Perch

Southern Flounder

Spotted Seatrout

Striped Mullet

Swordspine Snook

Tarpon

Tarpon Snook

Atlantic Needlefish

Strongylura marina

OTHER NAMES:

Agujon

RANGE: *Atlantic and Gulf coasts from New England to Texas.*

WHERE TO FISH: *Needlefish are easily spotted at the surface, anywhere from the open sea to far up freshwater streams, but are not often fished for, except occasionally for bait. Fished for or not, they often harass natural baits and are sometimes hooked and landed.*

DESCRIPTION: Green to blue back with silvery, translucent sides. Slender body. Long upper and lower bills are equipped with many sharp teeth.

SIZE: From a few inches to about 2 feet. World record 3 pounds, 4 ounces.

FOOD VALUE: Poor; not much there.

GAME QUALITIES: Frantic, sometimes acrobatic fighter, but lacks strength.

TACKLE: Any light or ultralight gear.

LURES AND BAITS: Any sort of cut bait or small live bait. Small spinners and minnow baits draw strikes and they can be caught on streamer flies.

Atlantic Stingray

Dasyatis sabina

DESCRIPTION: Whip-like tail has a barbed spike near base that is capable of administering a painful and sometimes dangerous wound. The body is flat with pointed head and "wingtips." Color is brown to almost black on top, and white on the underside.

SIZE: Usually 2-3 feet in "wingspan." Although much larger individuals are sometimes seen in marine environments, such monsters are not likely to be encountered upriver. World record 10 pounds, 12 ounces.

FOOD VALUE: Very good. The back and thick parts of wings taste like scallops.

GAME QUALITIES: Although not great fighters, they stick to bottom like a suction cup and cause the angler to work up a sweat.

TACKLE: Heavier baitcasting and spinning outfits; light saltwater gear.

LURES AND BAITS: Rays will take nearly any dead bait, whether of fish or crustacean origin.

OTHER NAMES:

Stingaree

RANGE: *From New England around Florida to Texas. Roams far upstream in many coastal rivers.*

WHERE TO FISH: *Over soft-bottom shallows and around sandbars. Hooked Rays must be handled very carefully to avoid the spiked tail.*

Atlantic Tomcod

Microgadus tomcod

Tommie
Tommie Cod

RANGE: *Labrador to Chesapeake Bay. Runs far inland in many streams and is sometimes landlocked.*

WHERE TO FISH: *Likes hard bottom with scattered rocks or debris. Many are taken from docks and jetties.*

DESCRIPTION: Color is olive or brown on the back and sides, yellowish below. Liberally mottled with slightly darker shadings. Fins are high and prominent and the tail is rounded.

SIZE: Averages 12 inches or less and reaches perhaps 16 inches.

FOOD VALUE: Excellent.

GAME QUALITIES: Cooperative but not a strong fighter.

TACKLE: Anything goes, from handlines and poles to sophisticated gear. Light spinning is best for sport.

LURES AND BAITS: Eats about any popular bait, such as clam, squid, cut fish and marine worms.

Bairdiella

Bairdiella icistia

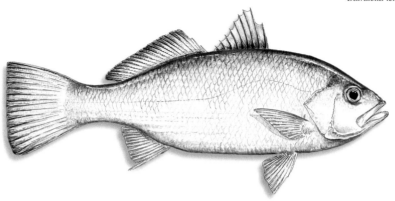

DESCRIPTION: The overall color is silvery and the mouth is small. Tail is square. Absence of canine teeth and very large spine on the anal fin distinguish it from juvenile Corvina.

SIZE: Averages around 8 inches long; occasionally reaches twice that length.

FOOD VALUE: An excellent panfish.

GAME QUALITIES: Cooperative but not too tough.

TACKLE: Pole, light spinning.

LURES AND BAITS: Worms make best natural bait, but minnows and cut fish are good. Some are taken on tiny jigs and other small lures.

OTHER NAMES:

Croaker

RANGE: *Pacific Coast and, like the Orangemouth Corvina, introduced into the Salton Sea.*

WHERE TO FISH: *Plentiful near shore in warm weather. Goes deeper when water temperatures drop.*

Bull Shark

Carcharhinus leucas

OTHER NAMES:

Freshwater Shark
Ground Shark
Cub Shark

RANGE: *While many species of sharks may briefly enter fresh water at the mouths of rivers, the Bull is the only one that roams far inland for extended periods of time. Its inland appearances in the United States have occurred mostly in Gulf Coast rivers from Southwest Florida to Louisiana, but in salt water it ranges from the Gulf to New England. The Bull is considered a dangerous shark, and has been blamed for deadly attacks along the Atlantic and Gulf coasts as well as in Central and South America.*

WHERE TO FISH: *Patient bottom fishing with large dead baits might get the angler connected with a Bull Shark in the lower reaches of Gulf rivers. Farther upriver, an occasional Bull may be present, but the odds of success diminish.*

DESCRIPTION: Brown or gray above with white underparts. The snout is short and rounded. An obvious feature is the large dorsal fin, located well forward—above the pectoral fins.

SIZE: Attains a weight of around 500 pounds, but most specimens are in the 100- to 200-pound class. World record 636 pounds, 14 ounces.

FOOD VALUE: Good.

GAME QUALITIES: A very strong and tenacious fighter.

TACKLE: Saltwater tackle with lines testing 30 pounds and up.

LURES AND BAITS: Best bait is a whole dead fish weighing a pound or two and slashed several times to increase smell appeal.

Common Snook

Centropomus undecimalis

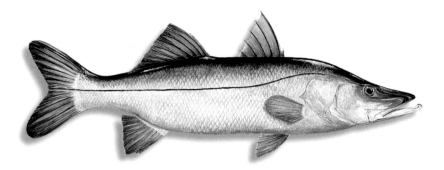

DESCRIPTION: A jet-black stripe along the lateral line makes a Snook easy to spot. Other trademarks are a tapered snout, long lower jaw and large, yellow fins.

SIZE: Average is about 3 to 15 pounds. Many juveniles weighing under 2 pounds are caught in fresh water, but big fish roam far inland as well. The usual maximum is around 30 pounds, but rare fish to 40 or more are taken. World record 53 pounds, 10 ounces.

FOOD VALUE: Excellent.

GAME QUALITIES: One of the best. Snook are both strong and acrobatic. Worst of all—from the angler's point of view—they are masters at fouling lines around any obstructions in the immediate area.

TACKLE: For Snook of decent size, use strong baitcasting or spinning rods, and rather heavy casting lines. Fly fishermen need No. 8 outfits or heavier, with stout leaders and heavy tippets. Light saltwater tackle is also used for trolling in the rivers, or for bait fishing.

LURES AND BAITS: Surface plugs and large streamer flies and poppers provide the most heart-stopping action when casting to shorelines. Plugs, jigs and spoons also get lots of strikes. Live fish and shrimp make the best natural baits. Small dead fish or chunks of larger fish can be fished on bottom with effect.

OTHER NAMES:

Lineside
Robalo
Sea Pike

RANGE: *South Florida and southeastern Texas; stragglers may be found in other Gulf States. In Florida especially, Snook are common in fresh water usually in rivers but frequently in landlocked lakes, ponds and backwaters. They also have been stocked experimentally in freshwater lakes, where they fare well but do not reproduce.*

WHERE TO FISH: *In fresh water, the great majority of snook hang close to snags or along shore around roots and undercuts. They also like deep, eddying pools, especially in cold weather.*

Fat Snook

Centropomus parallelus

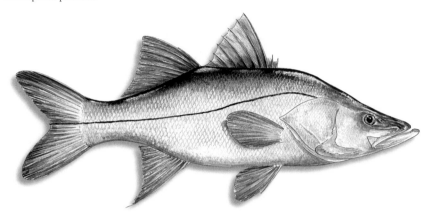

OTHER NAMES:

Cuban Snook
Calba

RANGE: *South Florida. Not common.*

WHERE TO FISH: *A target of opportunity in small streams, canals and backwaters.*

DESCRIPTION: Coloration is about the same as the Common Snook's, but the body is proportionately shorter and deeper.

SIZE: Rarely reaches Florida's legal minimum size of 26 inches. Most catches are in the 12- to 18-inch category. World record 9 pounds, 5 ounces.

FOOD VALUE: Excellent but seldom eaten because of length limits.

GAME QUALITIES: Pound for pound, as good as its bigger relative, the Common Snook, and equally adept at fouling lines on snags and roots.

TACKLE: Sporty on light spinning, baitcasting and fly gear.

LURES AND BAITS: Small surface and underwater plugs, spoons, jigs, live shrimp, live baitfish.

Gray Snapper

Lutjanus griseus

DESCRIPTION: Typical color is gray to dark green above with white underparts. Most specimens have an overall reddish cast. A black line runs from the snout to the dorsal fin, bisecting the eye. This line darkens perceptibly when the fish is excited or pursuing food.

SIZE: The average size in fresh water is 6-8 inches, occasionally 10 or 12 inches. Offshore, they frequently run to 5 pounds and can reach perhaps 20 pounds. World record 17 pounds.

FOOD VALUE: Excellent.

GAME QUALITIES: A hard striker and strong fighter, limited only by size.

TACKLE: Pole, light spinning, light baitcasting, sometimes fly.

LURES AND BAITS: In murky water, Snappers usually bite on live shrimp, pieces of shrimp, cut baits and small lures such as jigs and tiny crankbaits. Streamer flies also work well. This is one of the most cautious of fish, and in clear water, it may sometimes hold out for small live minnows or shrimp, fished on thin monofilament line.

OTHER NAMES:

Mangrove Snapper

RANGE: *Although found in salt waters of all southern coastal states, it commonly enters fresh water only along both coasts of Florida.*

WHERE TO FISH: *Sticks close to rocks, oyster bars, submerged limbs or mangrove roots.*

Ladyfish

Elops saurus

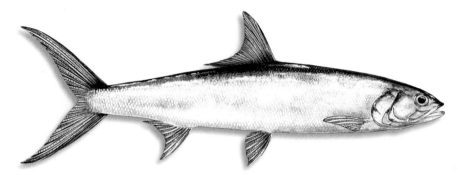

Skipjack
Chiro
Ten-Pounder

RANGE: *Most common, especially in fresh water, from Florida to Texas. The nearly identical Pacific Ladyfish is sometimes taken in the Colorado River.*

WHERE TO FISH: *In fresh water, Ladyfish might be found almost anyplace where bait schools are present. They frequently school and follow the food supply.*

DESCRIPTION: Silvery overall with a greenish back and single large dorsal fin, deeply forked tail and large, scoop-shaped lower jaw.

SIZE: Common at 1-2 pounds. Sometimes reaches 4 pounds or more and has been reported to 7 pounds. The archaic name "Ten-Pounder" is a mystery. World record 6 pounds.

FOOD VALUE: Poor. Flesh is soft and very bony.

GAME QUALITIES: Among the best fighters in their size class, Ladyfish jump frequently and can also get off some surprisingly long runs.

TACKLE: Light spinning, baitcasting and fly tackle provide the best sport.

LURES AND BAITS: Small topwater plugs, popping bugs and streamer flies, shallow-running spoons, jigs and small crankbaits all are productive artificial lures. Ladies will hit almost any natural bait of appropriate size, live or dead.

Orangemouth Corvina

Cynoscion xanthulus

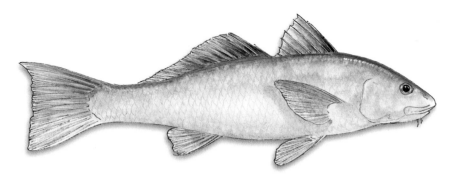

DESCRIPTION: Slender and streamlined in the manner of the Seatrouts. The back is tan with sides and belly silvery to white. Interior of the mouth is yellow to orange, and canine teeth are large. The tail is slightly pointed in the center. Fins are often yellow.

SIZE: Averages 2-6 pounds or so. Fish to 10 pounds are common and larger specimens are not unusual. Potential is to 30 or even 40 pounds. World record 54 pounds, 3 ounces.

FOOD VALUE: Excellent.

GAME QUALITIES: A showy and fairly strong fighter.

TACKLE: Spinning and baitcasting.

LURES AND BAITS: Live baitfish, particularly Tilapia are best bet, but many artificial lures produce too, especially spoons, jigs and swimming plugs.

RANGE: Pacific Coast from California to Central America. Heavily fished only in the Salton Sea, a large, saline lake in southern California, where it was introduced in the 1950s.

WHERE TO FISH: Spends much of its time in open water, where trolling is the best approach, but often feeds near shore, where it is accessible to pier fisherman.

Red Drum

Sciaenops ocellatus

OTHER NAMES:

Redfish
Red Bass
Channel Bass
Puppy Drum

RANGE: *The Atlantic and Gulf coasts from New York to Texas.*

WHERE TO FISH: *Red Drum adapt to fresh water and have been stocked in reservoirs in several states. They do not reproduce, however, and the angling impact has not been dramatic. The story is different, however in fresh waters that have access to the sea. Reds roam rivers and marshes freely over much of their range, but especially along the Gulf Coast.*

DESCRIPTION: The back and sides are brick red to dark bronze, and the belly is white. Small fish may be pinkish, or even nearly colorless. A dark, ringed spot or ocellus is present at the base of the tail on most fish. Some specimens, however, have more than one spot, often three or four and occasionally a cluster. Rare fish have no spot.

SIZE: The majority of catches, especially in fresh water, run from several pounds to 8 or 10 pounds. At sea, individuals to 30 pounds are not unusual, and potential size is huge from 50 pounds up to nearly 100. World record 94 pounds, 2 ounces.

FOOD VALUE: Fish to about 10 pounds are excellent. Larger ones tend to coarseness and often are protected by law.

GAME QUALITIES: A terrifically rugged fighter with great strength and stamina. Surface thrashing tactics are a part of nearly every battle, though Reds seldom jump.

TACKLE: Spinning and baitcasting serve best in fresh water, with some action available to the patient fly fisherman.

LURES AND BAITS: Crabs, shrimp and small baitfish top the list of live baits. Cut baits and dead crustacean baits are often just as good. Many artificial lures are very productive, including spoons, jigs, swimming plugs and topwater plugs.

Sargo

Anisotremus davidsoni

DESCRIPTION: Overall silver with a yellowish tinge and one prominent black bar extending downward on the side from under the dorsal fin to about the pectoral fin. Thick lips.

SIZE: Fish weighing 1-2 pounds are common; sometimes exceeds 3 pounds.

FOOD VALUE: Very good.

GAME QUALITIES: Tough fighter but small.

TACKLE: Pole, light spinning and baitcasting.

LURES AND BAITS: Lures seldom produce. Shrimp, crab, worms and cut baits are good bets.

OTHER NAMES:

Grunt
China Croaker

RANGE: *Pacific Coast from Central California to Baja, Mexico. Another Salton Sea import that has become an angling fixture.*

WHERE TO FISH: *Best spots are close to shore around brush and other structure. Many are taken from jetties and docks.*

Sheepshead

Archosargus probatocephalus

OTHER NAMES:

Convict Fish
Baitstealer

RANGE: *Most of the Gulf and East coasts, where it roams far into fresh water.*

WHERE TO FISH: *Around docks, pier pilings, shell bars or, in fact, nearly any hard-bottom areas where crabs hide or barnacles grow. In fresh water they like to hunt among rocks and roots for crayfish.*

DESCRIPTION: Vertical black bands on a white, gray or yellowish background identify the Sheepshead to most anglers, but its set of heavy, protruding teeth account for is name. The tail is forked. Spines of the dorsal and anal fins are strong and sharp.

SIZE: Common at about 1-7 pounds. Fish to 10 pounds are possible. World record 21 pounds, 4 ounces.

FOOD VALUE: Excellent, possibly because of their shellfish diet.

GAME QUALITIES: A challenge to hook because of its gentle bite, but a very tough fighter that uses its broad side to good advantage.

TACKLE: Stout-tipped baitcasting and spinning outfits. Poles are often used around pilings.

LURES AND BAITS: Sheepshead take artificial jigs or flies at times, but the serious seeker of Sheepshead always uses natural baits, most often crustaceans such as live shrimp, fiddler crabs (or any other small crab), crayfish or bits of blue crab. The meat of oysters, mussels and clams is productive too, as are marine worms.

Silver Perch

Bairdiella chrysoura

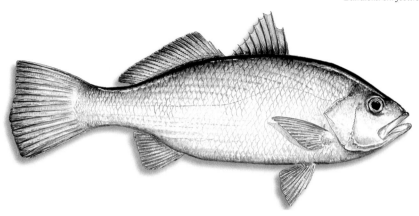

DESCRIPTION: Color is steel blue or gray on the back, silvery on sides and belly. Fins and tail are yellowish. Lack of canine teeth distinguish it from Seatrout.

SIZE: Averages around 6 inches; rarely over 10 inches.

FOOD VALUE: Excellent panfish.

GAME QUALITIES: Not much fight, but action is fast.

TACKLE: Lightest spinning gear.

LURES AND BAITS: Small pieces of shrimp and cut fish are greedily taken. Tiny jigs are a poor second to natural baits.

OTHER NAMES:

Silver Trout
Yellowtail

RANGE: The eastern version of the Bairdiella, this little fellow is common in many estuaries along the Atlantic and Gulf coasts. It roams far up coastal rivers and streams during the coldest times of year.

WHERE TO FISH: Silver Perch often school densely in deep holes and around bends of rivers.

Southern Flounder
Paralichthys lethostigma

OTHER NAMES:

Southern Fluke
Flattie

RANGE: *From North Carolina to Central Florida (both coasts) and west to Texas. Rare in South Florida. Frequently roams into fresh water in most rivers of its range.*

WHERE TO FISH: *Best in shallow coastal areas or riverine shorelines, but it is commonly taken from channels as well. Likes soft bottom close to rubble, rocks or bridge pilings.*

DESCRIPTION: Left-eyed. Color is brownish overall but heavily mottled with tan and white. Dark blotches on dorsal fin.

SIZE: Averages 2-4 pounds but is common up to about 6 pounds and sometimes exceeds 10 pounds. World record 20 pounds, 9 ounces.

FOOD VALUE: Excellent.

GAME QUALITIES: Hard striker and strong fighter.

TACKLE: Light spinning and baitcasting.

LURES AND BAITS: Live minnows and live shrimp work best, but dead baits are taken. Jigs are the most effective lures.

Spotted Seatrout

Cynoscion nebulosus

DESCRIPTION: Streamlined shape with large mouth, prominent canine teeth and dark gray back. Sides are usually silvery but may take on a gold hue in fresh water. Dark spots are sprinkled liberally over the upper sides, dorsal fin and tail.

SIZE: Most catches weigh 1-3 pounds, but 6-pounders are reasonably common in many areas and the potential is to 10 or more. Huge specimens, however, are not likely to be found in fresh water. World record 17 pounds, 7 ounces.

FOOD VALUE: Very good.

GAME QUALITIES: Not powerful, but a showy fighter that tugs hard and thrashes the surface.

TACKLE: Spinning and baitcasting outfits. Fly tackle with (in deep situations, such as most river fishing) sinking lines.

LURES AND BAITS: Live shrimp and live small fish, and strips of cut fish head the list of baits. Best lures in fresh water are sinking plugs, plastic-tailed jigs, and shrimp imitators, worked very slowly. Popping corks often enhance jig fishing.

OTHER NAMES:

Trout
Speckled Trout
Spotted Weakfish
Speck

RANGE: *Atlantic and Gulf coasts from New York to Texas. Generally enters freshwater rivers only in winter, but in some parts of Florida and Louisiana it can be caught in backwater areas all year.*

WHERE TO FISH: *In fresh water, most Trout are taken in deep areas where they seek refuge from the cold. They tend to be less active at these times and will respond best to very slow retrieves, or slow-trolling, or still fishing with natural bait.*

Striped Mullet

Mugil cephalus

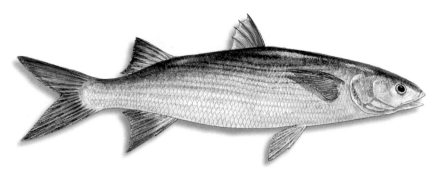

OTHER NAMES:

Black Mullet
Jumping Mullet

RANGE: *This is the saltwater fish most often seen in fresh waters of the Southeast, but it is also found in southern California and in the Colorado River. In the East, it ascends rivers from Virginia to Texas, often traveling long distances upstream. Landlocked populations occur.*

WHERE TO FISH: *Mullet are easier to catch on a hook in fresh water than in salt. They are constantly moving and feeding, though, and it takes patient float watching to hook them. Anglers concentrate their efforts along open shorelines of rivers, as well as around docks, seawalls and low bridges.*

DESCRIPTION: Back and upper sides are dark gray, the lower sides silvery, and the belly white. Several longitudinal stripes usually present. The mouth is small and triangular, and the tail deeply forked. Scales are large.

SIZE: Averages 1 or 2 pounds, but frequently reaches 4 pounds. World record 6 pounds, 15 ounces.

FOOD VALUE: Excellent. Note, however, that Mullet caught in fresh water are likely to have a musty or "muddy" taste unless skinned.

GAME QUALITIES: Wild and frantic, but not much stamina.

TACKLE: Poles work best. Spinning gear can be used. Fly fishermen with the patience of Job can hook them by tossing a small sinking fly into a feeding school and striking as soon as they visually observe the fly being sucked in.

LURES AND BAITS: Mullet are plankton feeders, so the popular baits are actually lures. The Mullet sucks them in, checks them for microscopic nutrients, and spits them out in the blink of an eye. The hook must be set at the first wiggle of the float. Pieces of bacon, kernels of corn, doughballs and even small bits of white plastic worm all have supporters among Mullet fishermen.

Swordspine Snook

Centropomus ensiferus

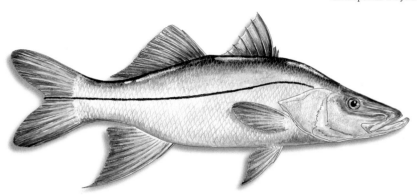

DESCRIPTION: Identifying feature is the long, robust spine on the front of the anal fin. This spine is prominent and sharp on all Snooks, but only on the Swordspine does it reach all the way to the tail fin when folded back. Otherwise, the Swordspine could pass, at a quick glance, for other Snook species.

SIZE: Seldom longer than a foot. World record 1 pound, 5 ounces.

FOOD VALUE: Insignificant.

GAME QUALITIES: It tries hard and shows off its jumps.

TACKLE: Ultralight spinning or pole.

LURES AND BAITS: Small jigs, spoons, live shrimp, live minnows.

OTHER NAMES:

Little Snook

RANGE: South Florida.

WHERE TO FISH: Most common in canals and around bridges that span quiet water.

Tarpon

Megalops atlanticus

OTHER NAMES:

Silver King
Sabalo

RANGE: *Although their range covers the entire Gulf Coast and much of the Atlantic seaboard, Tarpon roam fresh water mostly in the lower half of Florida. Small ones often are landlocked in Florida canals and ponds, while big fish roam the larger rivers, coastal streams and backwater areas. Freshwater anglers also encounter tarpon at times from the Florida Panhandle and Mobile Bay west to the Mexican border.*

WHERE TO FISH: *Tarpon can generally be spotted in open water as they roll at the surface. In rivers, they rest in deep holes but often feed in nearby shallows of coves and backwaters. Idly rolling Tarpon in rivers are notoriously picky strikers that usually hit best when lures or baits are presented down deep. In the shallows, topwater lures often coax strikes.*

DESCRIPTION: Bright silver is the dominant color, although the back is green and the forked tail dark. The mouth is large, with underslung, scoop-shaped lower jaw. The scales are large and thick. A filament or streamer extends from the last ray of the dorsal fin.

SIZE: Common in many sizes from a foot long to well over 100 pounds. Trophy fish can run from 150 to 250 pounds. World record 283 pounds.

FOOD VALUE: Poor.

GAME QUALITIES: Tarpon are very strong and resist doggedly, especially when in deep water, but they rely mostly on their jumping ability to shed an angler's hook. Usually they leap often and spectacularly.

TACKLE: Since Tarpon come in all sizes, all sizes and styles of tackle have a place, even fly tackle of trout dimensions when fishing protected fresh water for juvenile fish that average only a pound or two in weight. For bigger fish, stout baitcasting, fly and spinning tackle are all popular and appropriate, but saltwater gear is also used with natural baits.

LURES AND BAITS: Casters may do best with stout crankbaits fitted with extra-strength hooks. Topwater plugs, jigs and spoons should also be in the caster's arsenal. Bait fishermen prefer live small fish, live crabs and live shrimp. The bait, however, does not have to be live to get action. Tarpon eagerly scoop dead baits from the bottom.

Tarpon Snook

Centropomus pectinatus

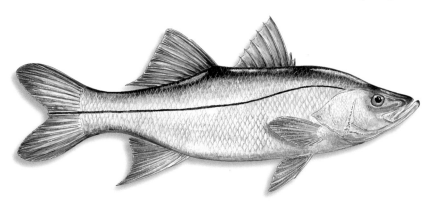

DESCRIPTION: The name comes from the similarity of the head to that of a small Tarpon. The body is flattened and not as robust as other Snooks.

SIZE: Usually a foot or so, but can reach at least 20 inches. World record 3 pounds, 2 ounces.

FOOD VALUE: Insignificant.

GAME QUALITIES: A lightweight among Snooks, but very acrobatic if it has the chance to perform.

TACKLE: The lightest casting tackle of any type.

LURES AND BAITS: Small jigs and spoons are good, as are live shrimp and live minnows.

RANGE: *South Florida.*

WHERE TO FISH: *It likes to stay well back in the roots of flooded river shorelines, but can also be encountered in canals and ponds of urban areas.*

One of the largest families of freshwater fishes in the world, Cichlids are native to Africa and Latin America, with only the Rio Grande Perch naturally found as far north as the United States. Native or not, however, Cichlids of various kinds are common in many parts of the country, and becoming more common and more varied all the time. Tropical fish dealers and collectors have been the source of most introductions, especially in Florida where a hodgepodge of Cichlid species now thrive. Most species are highly opportunistic and a few have even managed to overcome their tropical background to make themselves at home in more temperate waters. Some of the introductions have been accidental and some deliberate (to rid aquariums of excess specimens). Only one species of Cichlid has been reared and stocked as a gamefish. That is the Butterfly Peacock Bass, introduced by Florida's state fishery agency to the canals of South Florida, where it has become not only a major sporting target but also a biological control that helps reduce the ever-expanding number of other Cichlid species. While the Peacock Bass is a hefty fish, the Rio Grande Perch, and most of our transplanted Cichlids are rather small and all of them that are fishable are generally considered panfish. Some species—the Oscar being a prime example—are predatory and will aggressively strike many natural baits and artificial lures, but others have diets that do not include anything an angler might offer.

The Cichlids

Black Acara

Blackchin Tilapia

Blue Tilapia

Jaguar Guapote

Mayan Cichlid

Midas Cichlid

Mozambique Tilapia

Oscar

Peacock Cichlid

Redbelly Tilapia

Rio Grande Cichlid

Spotted Tilapia

Wami Tilapia

Black Acara

Cichlasoma bimaculatum

RANGE: *Southeast Florida from Lake Okeechobee southward.*

WHERE TO FISH: *Likes grassy areas with soft bottom in both residential and rural canals and connected ponds.*

DESCRIPTION: Similar to the Oscar in shape but much lighter color, being gray or whitish with dull vertical bands and dark spots on the side that link to form a jagged stripe. The tail is round, but the rear edges of the dorsal and anal fins are long and pointed.

SIZE: Seldom reaches 1 pound.

FOOD VALUE: Good.

GAME QUALITIES: A spunky panfish, but not as scrappy as the Oscar, with which it shares many waters.

TACKLE: Pole, ultralight spinning.

LURES AND BAITS: Earthworms and minnows are best baits. A few are caught on tiny spinners and sinking flies.

DESCRIPTION: Gold or orange on back and upper sides; pale blue below. Dark bars usually are present.

SIZE: Can run to 1 pound but most are less than a half pound.

FOOD VALUE: Good.

GAME QUALITIES: Spunky panfish but small.

TACKLE: Pole or light spinning.

LURES AND BAITS: Worms, cut fish, cut shrimp.

RANGE: Both coasts of Central Florida, especially Tampa Bay area and Cape Canaveral area. Also Hawaii.

WHERE TO FISH: Coastal streams and canals. Often encountered in brackish or even salty water.

Blue Tilapia

Tilapia aurea

OTHER NAMES:

Nile Perch

RANGE: *Plentiful in most areas of the Florida peninsula. Also introduced into several other states, including Alabama, Texas and Georgia, Colorado and Arizona.*

WHERE TO FISH: *Often spotted in shallow areas of lakes, but is not really fishable, since it seldom bites any sort of bait.*

DESCRIPTION: Color is powdery blue from back to lower sides, with white belly. Sides are marked by three or four dark vertical bars and scattered small spots.

SIZE: Common at 2-4 pounds. World record 4 pounds, 7 ounces.

FOOD VALUE: Excellent.

GAME QUALITIES: Hooked only rarely, but it has the size and strength to resist gamely if it happens.

TACKLE: Cast nets and bowfishing gear (where legal).

LURES AND BAITS: Eats algae and minute insect life. An occasional odd fish will take a worm, corn kernel or doughball.

Cichlasoma managuense

DESCRIPTION: This is another bass-like Cichlid, although much smaller than the Peacock Bass. Its body is thick and the dorsal and anal fins are pointed. Color is olive on the back, shading to gold with a purple sheen on the sides. Many small purple spots dot the sides, which may be marked with a row of black squares as well. The mouth is very large.

SIZE: Most weigh less than a pound but may run to 2 pounds. World record 3 pounds, 8 ounces.

FOOD VALUE: Tasty panfish.

GAME QUALITIES: Tough fighter for its size; strikes aggressively.

TACKLE: Pole, fly, ultralight spinning.

LURES AND BAITS: Hits a variety of artificials, headed by small spinners and surface plugs. Also takes streamer flies and popping plugs. Minnows and small shiners are the best natural baits.

RANGE: *Miami area of Florida and possibly expanding.*

WHERE TO FISH: *Around undercut edges of canals and rock pits, or near grass.*

Mayan Cichlid

Cichlasoma urophthalmus

OTHER NAMES:

Mayan Fish
Pez Maya

RANGE: *Native to Mexico. In the U.S., it is most common in the Everglades National Park of South Florida, although it extends northward to Miami and perhaps beyond.*

WHERE TO FISH: *Residential canals of Miami-Dade County, or in backcountry waters of Everglades National Park.*

DESCRIPTION: Yellow or gold with dark vertical bars. Throat and belly are red. Dorsal and anal fins are long and pointed.

SIZE: Averages perhaps a half-pound, but often exceeds 1 pound. World record 2 pounds, 8 ounces.

FOOD VALUE: Good panfish.

GAME QUALITIES: Feisty but small.

TACKLE: Light spinning and fly.

LURES AND BAITS: Small jigs, spoons, spinners, live shrimp.

Midas Cichlid

Cichlasoma citrinellum

DESCRIPTION: Coloration is highly variable. Adult males are usually golden with bars and other dark markings, but many are dull gray or white with black marks.

FOOD VALUE: Good.

GAME QUALITIES: Not big enough to resist much.

TACKLE: Pole, ultralight spinning.

LURES AND BAITS: More often seen than caught, they will bite worms or pieces of worm, doughballs, insect baits; rarely tiny spinners and artificial flies.

OTHER NAMES:

Golden Cichlid

RANGE: *Apparently limited to Miami-Dade County, Florida, but isolated catches reported elsewhere.*

WHERE TO FISH: *Around grass-beds and submerged cover in canals.*

Mozambique Tilapia

Tilapia mossambica

RANGE: *Best known in southern California, where it is the most common catch in the Salton Sea. Also established in Arizona, Florida and Southwest Texas.*

WHERE TO FISH: *Found both in open water and along shorelines.*

DESCRIPTION: Green or gray above, shading to greenish-yellow sides with three or four black spots. Underparts are yellow or white. Lips are large.

SIZE: Most weigh less than a pound, but 2-pounders are sometimes caught. World record 2 pounds, 8 ounces.

FOOD VALUE: Good.

GAME QUALITIES: Spunky panfish.

TACKLE: Pole, fly, spinning.

LURES AND BAITS: Takes the entire gamut of panfish baits, plus sinking flies, tiny spinners and jigs, and small popping bugs.

Oscar
Astronotus ocellatus

DESCRIPTION: Color is overall dark brown, but often with lighter orange bars or mottling. The ocellus—the black spot at the base of the tail—is black and ringed with red. There may be another spot or two on the dorsal fin as well. The body is thick and compressed.

SIZE: Averages around 8 ounces, although 1-pounders are not unusual. Oscars of 2 pounds or more are rare. World record 3 pounds, 8 ounces.

FOOD VALUE: Very good.

GAME QUALITIES: Very strong panfish; fights much like a Bluegill.

TACKLE: Pole, fly tackle, ultralight spinning.

LURES AND BAITS: Earthworms or small live minnows often produce long stringers, but Oscars are very aggressive and will hit both plastic worms and plugs of appropriate size, plus small spinners and topwaters. Fly fishermen take them on both popping bugs and small streamer flies.

OTHER NAMES:

Velvet Cichlid

RANGE: *The tip of Florida, from Lake Okeechobee southward. Also introduced in Hawaii. The Florida range continues to creep northward but is limited by colder water temperatures. Occasional catches are reported in other states but are almost surely of fish released from aquariums, not from any breeding population.*

WHERE TO FISH: *Likes still or sluggish water, with plenty of weeds.*

Peacock Cichlid

Cichla ocellaris

OTHER NAMES:

Peacock Bass
Butterfly Bass
Pavon

RANGE: *Native to South America, particulary the Amazon drainage. Dade and Broward counties, Florida (Miami-Fort Lauderdale area). A slight expansion of the range is possible, but is kept in check by the Peacock's rigid temperature requirements. Also established in Hawaii.*

WHERE TO FISH: *Canals and lakes, mostly in residential areas. Like the Largemouth Bass that share its waters, Peacocks usually stick close to ledges, structure or grassbeds.*

DESCRIPTION: Brightly colored, the Peacock is green to black on the dorsal surface with yellow or cream sides marked by vertical black bars. One large black spot, ringed in white, at the base of the tail is the "peacock eye" that gives the fish its common name. Large males have a longitudinal red stripe and a pronounced hump forward of the dorsal fin. The shape is bass-like, as is the large mouth.

SIZE: Averages 1-2 pounds, with numerous catches in the 3- to 5-pound range. Maximum is about 10 pounds. This is not the same species as the huge Peacocks so often reported from South America, but is a close relative that is better suited to a stateside environment. World record 12 pounds, 9 ounces.

FOOD VALUE: Very good, but most are released.

GAME QUALITIES: Outstanding. A hard striker and strong, acrobatic fighter, it is considered by most anglers to be a tougher customer than a Largemouth of similar size. Anglers also like the fact that Peacocks seldom bite at night or early in the morning, but prefer to feed in broad daylight.

TACKLE: Any tackle used for Black Bass, including fly rods.

LURES AND BAITS: Best bait is a live shiner, but Peacocks also hit just about every popular bass lure, with one glaring exception—they are not fond of plastic worms. Topwater plugs generally provide good action, as do popping bugs and big streamer flies for fly fishermen.

Redbelly Tilapia

Tilapia zilli

DESCRIPTION: Gray to dark green above with tan or light green sides. The sides are marked by several shadowy bars. The head is wider than the body. The entire underside is red.

SIZE: Averages 4-5 inches; occasionally to a foot or slightly longer.

FOOD VALUE: Very good.

GAME QUALITIES: Tough panfish.

TACKLE: Pole, spinning, sometimes fly.

LURES AND BAITS: Most panfish baits will work— small insects, worms, larvae and "homemade" baits, such as bread balls and corn.

RANGE: The Imperial Valley and nearby regions of southern California. Also found in southern Arizona and reported in Florida.

WHERE TO FISH: Drainage canals and streams hold the majority of these fish, but they also are caught in the Salton Sea.

Rio Grande Cichlid

Cichlasoma cyanoguttatum

OTHER NAMES:

Pearl Cichlid
Rio Grande Perch
Texas Perch

RANGE: *The only Cichlid native to the United States, it originally was found only in the Rio Grande and Nueces River systems of lower Texas but, with introductions, it now is found over much of the southern half of that state. Other introductions, both planned and accidental, have brought the fish to scattered other locations around the country, including Central Florida, Arizona, and even Illinois, where it is said to be doing well in the heated discharge waters of a power plant near Pekin.*

WHERE TO FISH: *Target shallow cover including grassbeds and brush.*

DESCRIPTION: Background color is bluish green—vivid on some fish, duller on others, depending on the waters where taken. In all cases, the entire fish, body and fins alike, is liberally sprinkled with turquoise dots. As with most Cichlids, adult males have a hump on the head.

SIZE: Most weigh 5 or 6 ounces. The Texas record is 1.5 pounds, but fish over 2 pounds are said to be fairly common in Mexico.

FOOD VALUE: Very good.

GAME QUALITIES: Scrappy fighter, much like a Bluegill.

TACKLE: Pole, ultralight spinning, fly.

LURES AND BAITS: All panfish baits work well, topped by earthworms, crickets and minnows. Small flies and poppers also take these fish, as do tiny spinners and Crappie jigs.

DESCRIPTION: Similar to the Black Acara, but vertical bands are more vivid and they continue onto the dorsal fin.

SIZE: Averages 4-5 inches; may reach a foot. World record 3 pounds.

FOOD VALUE: Good.

GAME QUALITIES: Spunky but small.

TACKLE: Pole or ultralight spinning.

LURES AND BAITS: Bites only occasionally, usually on a worm, cricket or doughball.

RANGE: *Mostly in Miami-Fort Lauderdale area of Florida, but also reported farther north, at least to Brevard County (Cape Canaveral area).*

WHERE TO FISH: *Ponds and still-water canals. Prefers soft bottom with grass for cover.*

DESCRIPTION: Very similar to Mozambique Tilapia, but lacks the white underside.

SIZE: Averages a half-pound or so; sometimes pushes 3 pounds.

FOOD VALUE: Good.

GAME QUALITIES: Zippy little fighter.

TACKLE: Pole, ultralight spinning, fly.

LURES AND BAITS: Takes the entire gamut of panfish baits, plus sinking flies, tiny spinners and jigs, and small popping bugs.

RANGE: *Southern California, but is not found in Salton Sea.*

WHERE TO FISH: *Still, weedy waters of canals, ponds and ditches.*

Eight species of Sturgeon are native to North America. Although one or more of them live in many of our large rivers, anglers in most areas usually don't realize it. Only the White, Green and Lake Sturgeons occur in fishable numbers; and even those are troubled in some parts of their range. The Atlantic, Shovelnose, Shortnose and Pallid Sturgeons can still be caught in various waters but are protected in most jurisdictions, and almost never targeted, although a few find their way onto lines meant for Catfish. Sturgeons are highly prized. The meat is tasty and the roe famous as caviar, but, even so, present-day Sturgeon fishermen release most of their catches. The real lure of angling for White and Lake Sturgeon is the chance of hooking a real giant, a fish weighing 100 pounds, or possibly even two or three times that weight. The White Sturgeon is the largest of our North American freshwater fishes, with specimens approaching one ton being taken in the past. Today's catches are far smaller. Still, 200-pounders remain common.

The Sturgeons

Atlantic Sturgeon

Green Sturgeon

Lake Sturgeon

Pallid Sturgeon

White Sturgeon

Shortnose Sturgeon

Shovelnose Sturgeon

Atlantic Sturgeon

Acipenser oxyrhynchus

OTHER NAMES:

Common Sturgeon
Eastern Sturgeon
Gulf Sturgeon

RANGE: *Atlantic Coast watersheds from Labrador to Central Florida. The Gulf Sturgeon, a subspecies, occurs along the Gulf Coast, from Tampa Bay, Florida to Lake Ponchartrain, Louisiana.*

WHERE TO FISH: *Not targeted because of depleted stocks.*

DESCRIPTION: Back and fins are dark gray, undersides whitish. Most obvious identifier is the snout, which is long and upturned.

SIZE: Historically, up to 15 feet and more than 1000 pounds. Largest at present probably are under 10 feet.

FOOD VALUE: Like most other sturgeons, excellent if available.

GAME QUALITIES: Strong fighter.

TACKLE: Heavy saltwater tackle.

LURES AND BAITS: Various cut baits and shellfish baits would work.

Green Sturgeon

Acipenser medirostris

DESCRIPTION: Color is dark green or olive green above, lighter green below. The snout is rather blunt and shovel-shaped. The barbels are usually closer to the mouth than to the snout.

SIZE: Can reach 7 feet and more than 300 pounds, although most catches are under 50 pounds.

FOOD VALUE: Poor.

GAME QUALITIES: The size alone makes it a challenge.

TACKLE: Heavy baitcasting, light saltwater or salmon mooching outfits.

LURES AND BAITS: Small baitfish, shrimp, cut fish, clams or doughball.

RANGE: *About the same as the White Sturgeon, but Green Sturgeon are less plentiful.*

WHERE TO FISH: *In estuaries and lower reaches of rivers, but the Green Sturgeon doesn't roam as far inland as the White Sturgeon.*

Lake Sturgeon

Acipenser fulvescens

RANGE: *Widely distributed in Canada south of Hudson Bay, from Manitoba eastward to Quebec; and in the U.S. from Minnesota to the Appalachians and south to Louisiana. Threatened in many areas; thriving in a few. Once common in many Great Lakes areas.*

WHERE TO FISH: *On sand or gravel bottom in clear water of both streams and lakes.*

DESCRIPTION: Usually brown in overall color, often quite dark. Snout is conical and sharp. Upper lobe of the tail is longer than the lower.

SIZE: On average, runs up to 30 pounds, although fish approaching 100 aren't uncommon. Fish 50 pounds are rare prizes, although the potential maximum is perhaps 200 or more. World record 168 pounds.

FOOD VALUE: Good, fresh or smoked.

GAME QUALITIES: Strong, dogged fighter that often jumps.

TACKLE: In the Lake Winnebago system of Wisconsin, spearing through holes in the ice is popular and legal. Elsewhere, traditional bottom fishing calls for heavy baitcasting gear, or heavy spinning outfits.

LURES AND BAITS: Natural baits such as small fish, cut fish, worms and crayfish.

Pallid Sturgeon

Scaphirhynchus albus

DESCRIPTION: Has the long, slim caudal peduncle of the Shovelnose Sturgeon, but the snout is shorter and more rounded and the color is lighter—light gray over white.

SIZE: Can reach perhaps 6 feet, but the norm is half that.

FOOD VALUE: Good.

GAME QUALITIES: A tough customer whose stamina is increased by swift water.

TACKLE: Bottom-fishing gear.

LURES AND BAITS: Mussels, crayfish, worms and other shellfish baits.

RANGE: The main channel of the Missouri River and the lower half of the Mississippi.

WHERE TO FISH: Prefers more turbid waters than the Shovelnose Sturgeon, but also is partial to strong current and hard bottom. It is much more uncommon than the Shovelnose, with which it shares much of its habitat. If caught, it is usually by anglers seeking other kinds of fish.

White Sturgeon

Acipenser stet

OTHER NAMES:

Pacific Sturgeon

RANGE: *Pacific Coast watersheds from southern Alaska to Central California. Best and best-known fishery is in the Columbia River. Although anadromous, some populations have become landlocked in the Columbia and other West Coast river systems because of dams.*

WHERE TO FISH: *On bottom. Fish gather in deeper holes to feed.*

DESCRIPTION: Color is brown or pale green above, dingy white below, and the fins are gray. The barbels are closer to the mouth than to the snout. No scutes are present behind the dorsal and anal fins.

SIZE: White Sturgeon are the largest fish in American fresh water, with specimens as heavy as 1800 pounds on record. Present-day catches, however, are mostly in the 50- to 300-pound range. World record 468 pounds.

FOOD VALUE: Large fish are released. Sturgeon of small (but legal) size are excellent, either fresh or smoked.

GAME QUALITIES: A rugged fighter that uses strength, stamina and dirty tricks, such as rolling in the line and leader. Often jumps.

TACKLE: Very heavy baitcasting gear or saltwater outfits.

LURES AND BAITS: Only natural baits are used. Leading the list are dead fish, such as shad, smelt, herring, trout and anchovies, along with cut fish, shrimp, clams, crayfish and earthworms.

Shortnose Sturgeon

Acipenser brevirostrum

DESCRIPTION: Sharing many waters with the Atlantic Sturgeon, this one is recognizable by its short and v-shaped snout, as well as average size. Coloration is similar.

SIZE: Averages around 2 feet; maximum perhaps 4 feet. World record 11 pounds, 2 ounces.

FOOD VALUE: Good.

GAME QUALITIES: Strong fighter.

TACKLE: Gear suitable for bottom fishing.

LURES AND BAITS: Clams, squid, shrimp, worms and cut fish are acceptable baits, but this Sturgeon too is rarely caught.

RANGE: New Brunswick and southern Quebec to North Florida.

WHERE TO FISH: Largely in estuaries and the lower reaches of rivers. Seldom ventures as far upstream as the Atlantic Sturgeon.

Shovelnose Sturgeon

Scaphirhynchus platorynchus

DESCRIPTION: This and the Pallid Sturgeon are similar and distinguishable from other Sturgeons by their long and slender caudal peduncles—the section just forward of the tail fin. The snout of the Shovelnose is long and upturned. Color is tan above, white below.

SIZE: A small Sturgeon, maximum 3 feet or less. World record 11 pounds, 2 ounces.

FOOD VALUE: Good.

GAME QUALITIES: Current makes them tough when hooked, despite modest size.

TACKLE: Gear suited to bottom fishing.

LURES AND BAITS: Mussels, crayfish, worms and other shellfish baits.

OTHER NAMES:

River Sturgeon

RANGE: The Mississippi River and its tributaries, from Pennsylvania west to Montana and south to Louisiana.

WHERE TO FISH: Strong current of river channels, over sand or gravel bottom. Sometimes caught by anglers seeking Catfish.

With their armor-like scales and long toothy bills, Gars look like holdovers from another age; and, indeed, they are, being among the most primitive of fishes. Not popular fishing targets; but they are familiar to a great many anglers because they are highly visible, staying at or near the top of the water much of the time. Their anatomy includes a rudimentary lung that supports the normal function of their gills and spurs them to roll at the surface to obtain supplemental air. Small Gar frequently pester fishermen by stealing baits and nipping at artificial lures while seldom getting hooked. A couple of species, however, have a following. One is the giant Alligator Gar, one of the largest predatory fish in North America; the other is the Longnose Gar, many of which have more than enough heft to provide exciting fishing. Gars are good table fare, although it is a task to remove the tasty flesh from the armored hide. Some cut steaks, then skin and clean the steaks individually.

The Gars

Alligator Gar

Florida Gar

Longnose Gar

Shortnose Gar

Spotted Gar

Alligator Gar

Lepisosteus spatula

OTHER NAMES:

Giant Gar

RANGE: *Gulf of Mexico and rivers from the Florida Panhandle to Mexico; also the Mississippi River drainage as far north as the Missouri and Ohio rivers.*

WHERE TO FISH: *Free-roaming but usually seen at the surface in backwater areas. Also ventures into coastal bays, and even the open Gulf.*

DESCRIPTION: The color usually is dark brown above, yellow below, with a thin stripe from head to tail. Usually identifiable by size alone, it also features an "alligator" snout—short and very wide. The Alligator Gar has two rows of teeth on each side, while other Gars have only one.

SIZE: Except for Sturgeons, this is the largest North American fish, sometimes reaching 10 feet and a weight of 300 pounds. The average is probably 25 to 75 pounds, but 100-pounders aren't rare. World record 279 pounds.

FOOD VALUE: Good.

GAME QUALITIES: A strong and roughhouse battler that often jumps.

TACKLE: Size dictates using saltwater tackle, or at least the heaviest baitcasting and spinning outfits.

LURES AND BAITS: Hits an artificial lure but is seldom hooked. Best baits are live and dead fish, presented near the surface under a float and on a sharp treble hook. Use a wire leader.

Florida Gar

Lepisosteus platyrhincus

DESCRIPTION: Similar to the Spotted Gar, but confusion can be avoided because their ranges don't overlap.

SIZE: Usually a couple of pounds, but a rare fish can run 10-20 pounds. World record 7 pounds, 8 ounces.

FOOD VALUE: Good but seldom eaten.

GAME QUALITIES: Big specimens fight.

TACKLE: Spinning, baitcasting, fly, pole.

LURES AND BAITS: Minnows, live or dead, plus worms and cut baits are good. Flies and small artificial lures are sometimes taken.

OTHER NAMES:

Garfish

RANGE: The Florida peninsula and southern Georgia.

WHERE TO FISH: Easy to spot at the surface in many drainage canals, streams, ponds and lakes.

Longnose Gar
Lepisosteus osseus

OTHER NAMES:

Garfish
Needlenose

RANGE: *From southern Quebec to Central Florida on the Atlantic shore, and from Tampa Bay to Mexico on the Gulf Coast. Found over most of the U.S. from the Rio Grande eastward.*

WHERE TO FISH: *Lives in streams as well as coastal estuaries and inlets, but rarely found in open salt water. Commonly seen rolling at the surface.*

DESCRIPTION: Brown or dark green on top and sides, cream or white underneath. Spots are scattered on the fins and, in some specimens, on the body.

SIZE: The largest Gar that's familiar to most anglers; it can grow to at least 6 feet and can weigh 50 pounds Most weigh 10 to 15 pounds. World record 50 pounds, 5 ounces.

FOOD VALUE: Good.

GAME QUALITIES: A wild fighter for a short time.

TACKLE: Spinning and baitcasting gear. Can be taken on flies.

LURES AND BAITS: Will hit a variety of artificials at times, but much more likely to bite natural baits like small fish or cut baits. Use wire leader and a treble hook.

Shortnose Gar

Lepisosteus platostomus

DESCRIPTION: Snout is shorter and broader than the other smaller Gars. Color is olive or brown above, fading to lighter brown or tan sides and cream-colored belly. Body and fins wear many brown or black spots. Spots on caudal, dorsal and anal fins, but seldom on body.

SIZE: Averages a couple of pounds; rarely tops 5 pounds. World record 5 pounds, 12 ounces.

FOOD VALUE: Edible, but little meat.

GAME QUALITIES: Modest.

TACKLE: Spinning, baitcasting, fly, pole.

LURES AND BAITS: Worms, minnows and small cut baits. Occasionally hits spinners or other artificial lures.

OTHER NAMES:

Garfish

RANGE: *The Mississippi River basin.*

WHERE TO FISH: *Likes quiet river backwaters and oxbows; also in lakes. Thrives in turbid water.*

Spotted Gar

Lepisosteus oculatus

DESCRIPTION: Brown above, tan or cream below. Many brown and black spots dot the sides and fins.

SIZE: Averages 2 to 4 pounds; sometimes reaches 10 pounds. World record 9 pounds, 12 ounces.

FOOD VALUE: Good but seldom eaten.

GAME QUALITIES: Modest.

TACKLE: Spinning, baitcasting, fly, pole.

LURES AND BAITS: Worms, minnows, and small cut baits are eagerly taken. Occasionally hits small artificial lures and popping bugs or streamer flies.

OTHER NAMES:

Garfish

RANGE: *From the Great Lakes south to the Gulf of Mexico, east to the Florida Panhandle, and west to Central Texas.*

WHERE TO FISH: *Likes quiet, clear water with vegetation. Found in lakes and streams.*

This chapter covers an assortment of species, most of which rank low on the prestige scale; yet some provide good sport to fishermen and, in some cases, good food as well. The Drum and the Bowfin are pretty tough gamesters that will strike artificial lures and give light tackle a thorough test. Both are nearly always encountered by anglers seeking more desirable species and so their gaming qualities often are overlooked. Others that are caught more often by accident than design include the Burbot of northern lakes and rivers, the Bigmouth Sleeper of southern waters, and the American Eel. The Eel claims a contingent of supporters, who seek it mostly for the table. The strange-looking Paddlefish is unique. Since it feeds only on plankton and cannot be coaxed into taking a bait, it must be caught by snagging. The Sea Lamprey is included here, representative of a large family of Lampreys that live in American waters. This particular one, an invader from the Atlantic Ocean, is the most familiar and also the most infamous, having at one time nearly decimated the fishery resources of the Great Lakes. Lampreys aren't hook-and-line targets, but many live in small streams and are useful as bait.

Chapter

A Miscellany

American Eel

Bigmouth Sleeper

Bowfin

Burbot

Chevron Snakehead

Freshwater Drum

Paddlefish

Sea Lamprey

American Eel

Anguilla rostrata

OTHER NAMES:

Common Eel

RANGE: *All Gulf and Atlantic drainages, from West Texas to Newfoundland and Labrador. More common near the coast, but it often roams far into the interior.*

WHERE TO FISH: *Occasionally caught in lakes but most often in flowing streams. Most likely caught at night.*

DESCRIPTION: The body is snakelike and the head pointed. The dorsal, caudal and anal fins are combined into one continuous fin. Color is dark gray to olive above; yellowish or white on the underside.

SIZE: Average is about 2 feet long, although some exceed 3 feet and a rare specimen may reach 5 feet. World record 9 pounds, 4 ounces.

FOOD VALUE: Good, especially when pickled or smoked.

GAME QUALITIES: A fair fighter that rolls and twists.

TACKLE: Most are caught at night by Catfish anglers on bait and spinning tackle.

LURES AND BAITS: Earthworms or cut bait.

Bigmouth Sleeper

Gobiomorus dormitor

DESCRIPTION: Long, cylindrical body with wide head, large mouth and round tail. Color is brown, mottled with yellow or tan.

SIZE: A pound or so on average; may reach 3 pounds.

FOOD VALUE: Good.

GAME QUALITIES: Not a battler.

TACKLE: Usually taken incidentally to Bass fishing on spinning or baitcasting gear.

LURES AND BAITS: Jigs, spoons, small crankbaits, live minnows.

OTHER NAMES:

Guabina
Rock Bass

RANGE: *This tropical species is found only in South Florida and Southwest Texas.*

WHERE TO FISH: *Rocks, ledges and undercuts of ponds, canals and slow streams.*

Bowfin

Amia calva

OTHER NAMES:

Mudfish
Blackfish
Grindle
Cypress Trout

RANGE: *Most of the eastern United States from the Great Lakes to the Gulf of Mexico.*

WHERE TO FISH: *Bowfins have rudimentary air-breathing capability and often are seen gulping air at the surface in still or even stagnant water. They often bite baits meant for other species— everything from worms aimed at panfish to live baits and large lures meant for Largemouth Bass.*

DESCRIPTION: Slender but stout body with long single dorsal fin and round tail. Color is dark brown, sometimes with yellowish patterns on the side. Many small, sharp, raspy teeth.

SIZE: The average is 2 to 5 pounds; fairly common at 6 to 8, and can top 20 pounds. World record 21 pounds, 8 ounces.

FOOD VALUE: Edible, but not often eaten.

GAME QUALITIES: A real brawler; very tough to land.

TACKLE: Baitcasting or spinning tackle.

LURES AND BAITS: Will hit any sort of live or cut bait and nearly any kind of artificial lure.

Burbot

Lota lota

DESCRIPTION: Identified by its long, slim shape, with a single barbel at the chin. The anal and second dorsal fins are long; the first dorsal being short. The tail is rounded. Color is dark brown on top, with mottled sides of lighter brown.

SIZE: Averages a foot to 18 inches long, but often reaches 10 pounds, and can grow to 15 pounds. World record 18 pounds, 11 ounces.

FOOD VALUE: Good.

GAME QUALITIES: Modest fighter.

TACKLE: Occasionally caught while fishing deep for Lake Trout with spinning or baitcasting gear, and on ice-fishing rigs.

LURES AND BAITS: Crustaceans or small fish; spoons and jigs.

OTHER NAMES:

Cusk
Eelpout
Ling
Lawyer

RANGE: *Widespread throughout Canada and the northern United States; it is one of two members of the Cod family found in fresh water, the other being the Tomcod. Likes deep water of big lakes and rivers.*

WHERE TO FISH: *It stays deep most of the year, but comes into shallows in the spring. A fairly common, if unintended, ice-fishing catch in some northern lakes.*

Chevron Snakehead

Channa striata

OTHER NAMES:

Pongee
Snakehead
Murel

RANGE: *Hawaii, primarily Lake Wilson (Oahu).*

WHERE TO FISH: *Shallow, grassy areas.*

DESCRIPTION: Slender body with pointed snake-like head. Dorsal and anal fins are long and the tail is oval-shaped. Color is dark brown or black above, lighter brown on the sides and yellowish below. Dark spots dot the sides, fins and gill covers.

SIZE: From a pound or so to about 3 pounds; occasionally to 5 pounds.

FOOD VALUE: Good.

GAME QUALITIES: Fairly tough, but no slugger.

TACKLE: Caught on Bass gear—spinning or baitcasting.

LURES AND BAITS: Natural baits are best—worms, live fish, cut baits—but Pongee also take artificial lures such as spinners, spoons and small plugs.

Freshwater Drum

Aplodinotus grunniens

DESCRIPTION: Identified not only by its grunting sounds. Its color is dark above and silvery on the sides. The body is arched and the tail pointed. The first ray of the pelvic fin sports a long filament.

SIZE: Commonly 2 to 10 pounds, sometimes topping 20 pounds. World record 54 pounds, 8 ounces.

FOOD VALUE: Fair.

GAME QUALITIES: Strong, determined fighter.

TACKLE: Usually caught by anglers casting with spinning or baitcasting gear, or fishing on the bottom.

LURES AND BAITS: Drum will hit almost any natural bait from worms to live shiners, and a great many artificial lures too.

OTHER NAMES:

Sheepshead
Croaker

RANGE: It has the widest natural range of any North American sportfish, stretching from the eastern slopes of the Rockies to near the Atlantic Coast, and from Hudson Bay, Canada, south to the Gulf of Mexico.

WHERE TO FISH: Drum prefer big waters. They school in the shallows during the summer, retreating to deep water in winter. Usually taken incidentally to fishing for other species, particularly walleye and bass.

Paddlefish

Polyodon spathula

OTHER NAMES:

Spoonbill
Shovelnose
Shovelnose Catfish

RANGE: *Mississippi River drainage, west to Montana and east to the Apalachians. Also other Gulf drainages from Texas to Mobile Bay.*

WHERE TO FISH: *It remains common in large rivers and some impoundments of Middle America. Most fishing takes place in tailwaters of dams.*

DESCRIPTION: No mistaking this fellow, with his large size, shark-like shape, huge mouth and paddle-shaped upper bill. Color is gray to black above, with light sides that are sometimes mottled. The belly is white.

SIZE: Most catches run 30 to 50 pounds, some as high as 80 or 90 pounds. Fish supposedly 150 pounds are on record.

FOOD VALUE: Excellent.

GAME QUALITIES: Tough because of size and swift water where it's usually taken and because snagged fish fight harder than those hooked in the mouth.

TACKLE: Heavy baitcasting or light saltwater gear, suitable for snagging with heavy weights.

LURES AND BAITS: A plankton feeder, the Spoonbill is caught only by snagging, using heavily weighted treble hooks.

Sea Lamprey

Petromyzon marinus

DESCRIPTION: Being the best known and the largest, this species is representative of numerous species of Lamprey in North America. All are similar in their Eel-like shape and the fact that they have cartilaginous skeletons and a sucking disk instead of a mouth. The Sea Lamprey is brown to olive above, with dark brown blotches on the sides.

SIZE: Can grow to more than 3 feet, although most are under 2 feet.

FOOD VALUE: Modest and not popular table fare.

GAME QUALITIES: None.

TACKLE: Nets.

LURES AND BAITS: None.

OTHER NAMES:

Lamprey Eel
Lamper

RANGE: The Sea Lamprey is found in many Atlantic rivers but is most notorious for its past depredations of fishes in the St. Lawrence Waterway and Great Lakes. Other species inhabit mostly small streams and brooks throughout North America.

WHERE TO FISH: Not fishable by sporting methods.

Suckers will never be ranked among the upper crust of game varieties, but they certainly are among the most numerous kinds of fish in fresh waters throughout the continent. Veteran anglers are familiar with suckers of one kind or another, even though they may never have hauled up a single one on the ends of their line. That's because they are often easy to spot in clear or low-water streams, or along the shallow perimeters of many lakes. Catching them, however, is a different matter. Not many fishermen even try, and those who do aren't likely to be successful unless they study the usual romping grounds or migratory paths of the fish and then practice patient bottom fishing. Folks with less patience might take them by spearing, snagging, or bowfishing. Regardless of species, Suckers usually are much more numerous in the spring when they stage spawning runs in streams. In all, more than 50 species of Suckers are found in North America, many of them within restricted ranges. As a class, Suckers make good eating, especially at spawning time; but only if you're willing to deal with many bones. Those covered here are representative of the group. The Buffalos attain large size, often exceeding 50 pounds in weight and sometimes topping 80 pounds.

The Suckers

Bigmouth Buffalo

Smallmouth Buffalo

Black Buffalo

Quillback

Longnose Sucker

Flannelmouth Sucker

White Sucker

Shorthead Redhorse

Blacktail Redhorse

River Redhorse

Golden Redhorse

Blue Sucker

Creek Chubsucker

Lake Chubsucker

Bigmouth Buffalo

Ictiobus cyprinellus

OTHER NAMES:

Buffalofish
Buffalo Sucker
Gourdhead
 Buffalo
Redmouth Buffalo

RANGE: Saskatchewan and Manitoba, Plains and western Great Lakes States, and Mississippi River drainages, east to Ohio and south to Louisiana.

WHERE TO FISH: Shallow areas with soft bottom and vegetation.

DESCRIPTION: The body is stout. Large head and "shoulders" account for the name "Buffalo." Color is olive to shiny brown above, dull greenish-yellow on the sides and white below.

SIZE: Average is about 2 to 10 pounds, but many fish run well over 20 pounds and the potential is to at least 80 pounds. World record 70 pounds, 5 ounces.

FOOD VALUE: Good, especially smoked.

GAME QUALITIES: Tough, Carp-like bulldogging battle. Big ones are a challenge.

TACKLE: Stout baitcasting or spinning gear. Catfish fishermen sometimes take them on trotlines.

LURES AND BAITS: Worms and various insects.

Smallmouth Buffalo

Ictiobus bubalus

DESCRIPTION: The body is compressed and humpbacked. The head's conical, with a small mouth that extends downward. Color is lighter than the Bigmouth Buffalo, usually being gray to bronze above, and light yellow on the sides.

SIZE: About the same as the Bigmouth Buffalo, on average about 2 to 10 pounds, but not commonly exceeding 50 pounds. World record 82 pounds, 3 ounces.

FOOD VALUE: Good.

GAME QUALITIES: Tough brutish battler.

TACKLE: Stout baitcasting or heavy spinning gear.

LURES AND BAITS: Worms and various insects.

OTHER NAMES:

Thick-lipped Buffalo
Razorback Buffalo
Highback Buffalo

RANGE: *About the same as the Bigmouth but extending farther into Texas, including Rio Grande drainage.*

WHERE TO FISH: *Likes rivers but is also found in lakes. Prefers deeper and clearer water than the Bigmouth. It is less plentiful and is not so often caught.*

Black Buffalo

Ictiobus niger

OTHER NAMES:

Lake Buffalo
Bluerooter
Mongrel Buffalo
Round Buffalo

RANGE: *Much less common than the other Buffalos, with a range covering the lower Great Lakes States and Plains States. Introduced farther west into waters of Texas and Arizona.*

WHERE TO FISH: *Slow pools, eddies, and backwaters of large rivers; shallow, grassy edges of lakes and impoundments.*

DESCRIPTION: Streamlined in shape, with high dorsal fin. Back is rounded rather than ridged, as in the Smallmouth Buffalo. Color is dark gray above, yellow or coppery on the sides, and white below.

SIZE: Not much different from the other Buffalos— good size on average, 2 to 10 pounds, with a top weight of more than 50. World record 63 pounds, 6 ounces.

FOOD VALUE: Excellent.

GAME QUALITIES: Big ones, especially, are strong and persistent battlers.

TACKLE: Stout baitcasting or heavy spinning gear.

LURES AND BAITS: Worms and various insects.

Quillback

Carpiodes cyprinus

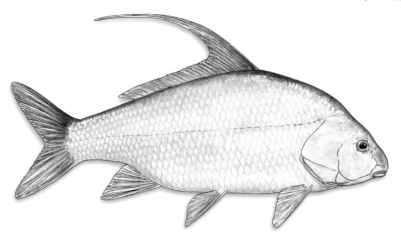

DESCRIPTION: This is one of several similar species of Carpsuckers, which are silvery and deep-bodied, with small, underslung mouths. The first few rays of the dorsal fin are high and elongated.

SIZE: Averages a couple of pounds; reaches 10 pounds on rare occasion. World record 6 pounds, 8 ounces.

FOOD VALUE: Good.

GAME QUALITIES: Modest.

TACKLE: Bottom-fishing gear.

LURES AND BAITS: Worms and Catfish baits occasionally trigger bites.

OTHER NAMES:

**White Carp
White Sucker
Highfin**

RANGE: *Most large rivers of Middle America. The Quillback is the only Carpsucker found in the Great Lakes and the western Canadian Provinces, principally Saskatchewan, Manitoba and Alberta.*

WHERE TO FISH: *Quillback graze river bottoms for microscopic food organisms. The few hook-and-line catches usually are made by anglers fishing on bottom for other species.*

Longnose Sucker

Catostomus catostomus

OTHER NAMES:

Finescale Sucker
Northern Sucker
Sturgeon Sucker

RANGE: *Widely distributed in northern areas, it is a cold-water species that covers Alaska and most of Canada, from Arctic drainages to the southern provinces. In the States, its strongholds are the Great Lakes region and New England, with smaller populations in Montana, Wyoming and Colorado.*

WHERE TO FISH: *Deep water of rivers and lakes most of the year; shallower during spawning runs of spring.*

DESCRIPTION: Snout extends beyond the mouth. Color overall is dark gray to dull green, with blotches along the upper sides, and white or yellowish belly. Spawning females are brighter, brassy, or dull gold.

SIZE: Around 12 inches long on average; sometimes to 2 feet. World record 6 pounds, 9 ounces.

FOOD VALUE: Good.

GAME QUALITIES: Modest.

TACKLE: Bottom-fishing gear.

LURES AND BAITS: Most hook-and-line catches are made with worms.

Flannelmouth Sucker

Catostomus latipinnis

DESCRIPTION: Shape is rather streamlined, and the caudal peduncle (that portion of the body just forward of the tail) is long and slim. Lower lip is exceptionally large and fleshy. Color is olive above, creamy below, with orange fins.

SIZE: Averages around a foot; grows to 18 inches or so. World record 2 pounds, 6 ounces.

FOOD VALUE: Good.

GAME QUALITIES: Not much.

TACKLE: Any bottom-fishing gear.

LURES AND BAITS: Bites fairly often on worms or other panfish and Catfish baits.

RANGE: The Colorado River basin of the southwestern United States.

WHERE TO FISH: Prefers riffles and rocky pools of larger streams and rivers.

White Sucker

Catostomus commersoni

OTHER NAMES:

Common Sucker

RANGE: *A Sucker with wide distribution, covering most of the lower half of Canada and the upper half or the United States east of the Rockies. Extends as far south as Tennessee and northern Georgia and Alabama.*

WHERE TO FISH: *This species is comfortable in just about any quality of water and any depth. It likes soft, sandy bottom near vegetation, and often roams shallow shorelines.*

DESCRIPTION: The body is cylindrical and the snout just extends beyond the mouth. Color is overall dull brown most of the time but brighter during the spawn, when lavender or pink tones may appear.

SIZE: Averages about a pound; rarely to 5 pounds. World record 6 pounds, 8 ounces.

FOOD VALUE: Fair to poor.

GAME QUALITIES: Modest.

TACKLE: Bottom-fishing gear.

LURES AND BAITS: Worms and insects.

Shorthead Redhorse

Moxostoma macrolepidotum

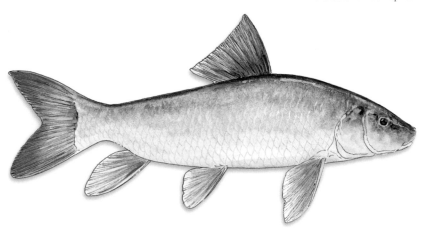

DESCRIPTION: Largest of the Redhorse group of Suckers that gets the name from their bright red or orange fins. A short, blunt head and large eye mark this species, which has a forked tail in which the upper lobe is slightly longer than the lower. Scales are large. Color is olive above, with yellow or brassy sides.

SIZE: Averages around 2 or 3 pounds; rarely exceeds 8 pounds. World record 8 pounds, 12 ounces.

FOOD VALUE: Good.

GAME QUALITIES: Fairly hard fighter.

TACKLE: Pole, spinning and baitcasting gear, used for bottom fishing.

LURES AND BAITS: Worms and various insects, such as crickets and larvae.

OTHER NAMES:

Northern Redhorse
Eastern Redhorse
Carolina Redhorse
Redfin Redhorse

RANGE: *In the United States, the Great Lakes and the Missouri and Mississippi River drainages as far south as Arkansas and Tennessee; also in Atlantic drainages from New York to South Carolina, but absent from most of New England. In Canada, the range extends from the St. Lawrence Waterway west to Saskatchewan and south of Hudson Bay.*

WHERE TO FISH: *Rocky bottom of clear, swift waters, and pools in such streams. Fares poorly in silty or muddy water.*

Blacktail Redhorse

Moxostoma poecilurum

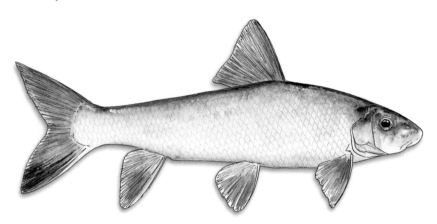

RANGE: *Gulf Coast rivers and streams from Galveston Bay, Texas to the Florida Panhandle.*

WHERE TO FISH: *Likes hard or sandy bottom of streams; also found in some lakes of the region.*

DESCRIPTION: Lower lobe of the tail fin is dark gray or black, but all other fins are red or orange. Body is cylindrical and nose blunt. Color is bronze above and white or yellowish on the sides, with gray belly.

SIZE: Most run about 1 pound; occasionally to about 5 pounds.

FOOD VALUE: Fair.

GAME QUALITIES: Modest.

TACKLE: Pole or light spinning gear.

LURES AND BAITS: Worms, insects, larvae.

River Redhorse

Moxostoma carinatum

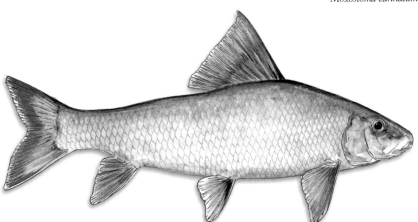

DESCRIPTION: Head is large and body stout. Lower lobe of the red tail is pointed, while the upper lobe is rounded. Color is greenish-gold above. Silvery on the sides. Crescent-shaped spots on sides. Bold black line down the side of breeding males.

SIZE: Average is 2 or 3 pounds, but is common to 5 pounds, and sometimes tops 10. World record 8 pounds, 11 ounces.

FOOD VALUE: Fair.

GAME QUALITIES: Modest.

TACKLE: Bottom-fishing gear.

LURES AND BAITS: Worms, crickets, larvae.

RANGE: *Central Mississippi basin. Gulf area from the Pearl River, Mississippi to the Escambia River in the Florida Panhandle. Present, but less common, in Great Lakes area and St. Lawrence drainage of Canada.*

WHERE TO FISH: *Likes the hard-bottom areas of clear streams, but some are found in lakes and reservoirs.*

Golden Redhorse

Moxostoma erythrurum

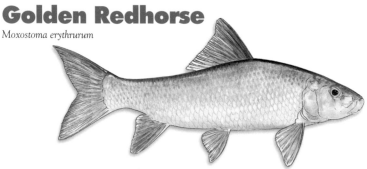

RANGE: *Mississippi River basin from New York and southern Ontario west to the Dakotas and south to Mississippi. Absent from Atlantic drainages.*

WHERE TO FISH: *This sucker prefers clear water and hard bottom. Found mostly in streams.*

DESCRIPTION: Bronze or brown above, with yellowish sides and white or cream belly. Scales on back are edged in black. The tail is pointed and both lobes are the same length. The dorsal fin is usually gray and concave. Other fins are orange or red. Large males may have a stripe along the side and a gray tail.

SIZE: Most catches run 2 or 3 pounds, but 5-pounders are common and they can grow to 10 or more. World record 4 pounds, 1 ounce.

FOOD VALUE: Fair.

GAME QUALITIES: Modest.

TACKLE: Bottom-fishing gear.

LURES AND BAITS: Worms, crickets, larvae.

Blue Sucker

Cycleptus elongatus

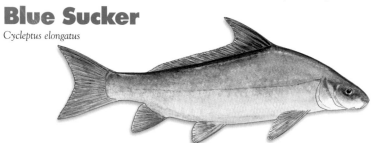

OTHER NAMES:

Missouri Sucker

RANGE: *Major rivers of the Midwest, from the Rio Grande to Mobile Bay, and north to the Missouri and Ohio River drainages.*

WHERE TO FISH: *Prefers clear water with rocky or hard bottom. Found mostly in the major streams and lower reaches of their tributaries; some occur in impoundments.*

DESCRIPTION: Blue or gray above; bluish-white below with dark blue fins. Body is long and tail forked. Head is small and blunt, and mouth is horizontal.

SIZE: Typically up to 18 inches, but may reach 3 feet on occasion.

FOOD VALUE: Fair.

GAME QUALITIES: Strong fighter.

TACKLE: Bottom-fishing gear.

LURES AND BAITS: Worms and aquatic insects.

Creek Chubsucker

Erimyzon oblongus

DESCRIPTION: The head is small and mouth tiny. Dorsal and anal fins are large and rounded. Tail is forked but lobes are rounded. Color is brownish above and white to yellow below. Blotches on side join to form an apparent stripe.

SIZE: Averages 6 or 8 inches but can exceed a foot in length.

FOOD VALUE: Modest.

GAME QUALITIES: Poor.

TACKLE: Pole.

LURES AND BAITS: Earthworms or pieces of crayfish. Feeds on small crustaceans and aquatic insects.

RANGE: *Atlantic states south to middle Georgia, and also the Mississippi drainage from the Gulf to the Great Lakes.*

WHERE TO FISH: *Likes headwaters of small streams and creeks, but some are found in lakes. Prefers gravel bottom close to vegetation.*

Lake Chubsucker

Erimyzon sucetta

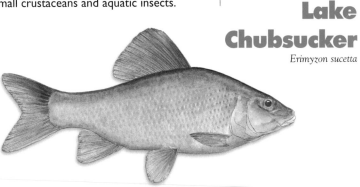

DESCRIPTION: Similar to the Creek Chubsucker but lacks the blotches on side. Young have a dark stripe on side which disappears with growth.

SIZE: Averages about 8 inches; grows to perhaps 18 inches.

FOOD VALUE: Poor.

GAME QUALITIES: Poor.

TACKLE: Lightest spinning gear.

LURES AND BAITS: Worms and insects.

RANGE: *Portions of the Mississippi drainage and across the Southeast from Louisiana to Virginia. Also in Texas.*

WHERE TO FISH: *Not common in streams. Inhabits lakes, ponds and marshes over silt or sand.*

Shads and Herrings belong to the same large family, the Clupeidae. Mooneye and Goldeye are similar in appearance but of a different group. Smelts are classified separately from either, but all the fish in this chapter have much in common when viewed from a fisherman's standpoint. The bigger ones are superb light-tackle gamefish, the smaller ones make great bait, and nearly all of them are fine eating. The American Shad is the leading gamester because of large size and spectacular, leaping fight. It stages annual spawning runs in rivers of both the Atlantic and Pacific coasts, frequently drawing hundreds of fishermen to one small stretch of the stream where they are concentrated. The American Shad is frequently referred to in books and magazine articles as "freshwater tarpon." Some of the other Shads are just about as spunky and acrobatic but lack the size and muscle to match the American Shad. All the Shads and Herring, however, do great service by providing forage for many game species and bait for anglers. When they are running, Smelt are easy to catch and maybe even easier on the palate. Goldeye and Mooneye are primarily northern species that can be easily caught on light gear and are good fighters, but are seldom sought by sportsmen who generally focus on more prestigious quarry.

Herrings, Shads, Smelts, and Mooneyes

Alewife

Alosa pseudoharengus

OTHER NAMES:

Branch Herring
Freshwater
Herring

RANGE: Atlantic coastal streams from Newfoundland to South Carolina; also the St. Lawrence Waterway and all the Great Lakes. Numerous other land-locked populations from Canada to Tennessee.

WHERE TO FISH: Spawns in the spring, but is not an angling target. Valued mostly as bait and chum.

DESCRIPTION: Blue or green above, with silver sides and faint dark longitudinal stripes. Body is fairly deep and rounded. Lower jaw does not extend beyond upper jaw when mouth is closed. Single spot just aft of gill cover.

SIZE: Averaging under 6 inches in fresh water, it can reach 16 inches or so in the sea and large rivers.

FOOD VALUE: Large ones are good, especially smoked or pickled.

GAME QUALITIES: None.

TACKLE: Nets are best, but sometimes hits small baited hooks or lures.

LURES AND BAITS: Bits of fish or cut shrimp; tiny flies on multiple bait rigs.

Blueback Herring

Alosa aestivalis

DESCRIPTION: Blue back and silvery sides. What appear to be faint stripes are actually raised scales. Small spot behind gill cover.

SIZE: Less than a foot on average but can reach about 16 inches.

FOOD VALUE: Good, especially pickled or smoked.

GAME QUALITIES: Some fun on the lightest tackle.

TACKLE: Ultralight spinning and light fly gear.

LURES AND BAITS: Can be caught on tiny hooks baited with bits of cut bait, or on multiple tiny flies rigged as bait-catching devices.

OTHER NAMES:

Summer Herring
Glut Herring
Blue Herring

RANGE: *Lower reaches of coastal rivers from Nova Scotia to Florida. Introduced into some reservoirs as well.*

WHERE TO FISH: *Prefers briskly flowing current over rock or shell bottom.*

Skipjack Herring

Alosa chrysochloris

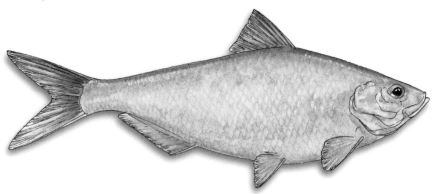

OTHER NAMES:

Golden Shad

RANGE: *Mississippi River and its larger tributaries as far north as South Dakota. Also other Gulf Coast rivers from the Apalachicola on the Florida Panhandle, to the Colorado in Texas.*

WHERE TO FISH: *Open water of large rivers and reservoirs.*

DESCRIPTION: Blue-green above is sharply separated from silver sides. Looks much like the Hickory Shad except for absence of the spot behind the gill cover.

SIZE: Averages a foot or less but can grow to 2 feet. World record 3 pounds, 12 ounces.

FOOD VALUE: Good, although very bony.

GAME QUALITIES: Acrobatic, with jumps and splashes.

TACKLE: Light fly or spinning.

LURES AND BAITS: Small lures, streamer flies, spinners, spoons. Also live minnows.

American Shad

Alosa sapidissima

DESCRIPTION: Color is green above with silvery sides. A dark spot just behind the gill cover is followed by a line of smaller black dots. Sharp ridge on the belly.

SIZE: Average is from 2 to 4 pounds, but a few run to 8 or 10 pounds. World record 11 pounds, 4 ounces.

FOOD VALUE: Excellent but bony; roe is a delicacy.

GAME QUALITIES: Terrific battler and very acrobatic.

TACKLE: Spinning gear is the most popular, but Shad are favorites of many fly fishermen on both coasts.

LURES AND BAITS: Spin fishermen rely mostly on jigs called Shad darts or small spoons and jigs, often rigging them in a tandem setup. Both trolling and casting are popular. Flyrod anglers use flashy streamers, usually with sinking lines.

OTHER NAMES:

White Shad
Common Shad
Atlantic Shad
Alose

RANGE: Atlantic Coast rivers from Labrador to North Florida. Introduced to the Pacific Coast's Sacramento River in the late 1800s, it is now found in other rivers from Mexico to Alaska, but is most common from Central California to southern British Columbia.

WHERE TO FISH: Open water of larger rivers during spawning runs. The Shad is anadromous and invades rivers to spawn in the spring.

Hickory Shad

Alosa mediocris

OTHER NAMES:

Fall Herring

RANGE: *Atlantic Coast streams from Maine to North Florida.*

WHERE TO FISH: *Also anadromous, the Hickory Shad generally finds the smaller tributaries, but some mix with their larger relatives in big rivers.*

DESCRIPTION: Similar to the American Shad but smaller. The series of black dots is present but this fish is usually distinguishable by size, and always by the lower jaw, which is longer than the upper.

SIZE: Most run from a half pound to 1 pound. Maximum is around 3 pounds.

FOOD VALUE: Bony but rich and flavorful.

GAME QUALITIES: Matches other Shads except for size.

TACKLE: Ultralight spinning and light fly gear.

LURES AND BAITS: Tiny jigs, spoons and spinners; live minnows.

Alabama Shad

Alosa alabamae

DESCRIPTION: Similar to the Hickory Shad, but has only a single dot behind the gill cover. Geography, too, is a giveaway, since this is the only one of the larger Shads found in Gulf Coast drainages.

SIZE: Averages 1 pound or so; occasionally reaches 4 pounds.

FOOD VALUE: Very good but bony.

GAME QUALITIES: Small but exciting; jumps frequently.

TACKLE: Ultralight spinning and light fly gear.

LURES AND BAITS: Tiny jigs, spoons and spinners; live minnows.

OTHER NAMES:

Ohio Shad

RANGE: *Large Gulf Coast rivers from the Suwannee in Florida to the Mississippi.*

WHERE TO FISH: *Open water of rivers and larger tributaries.*

Gizzard Shad

Dorosoma cepedianum

RANGE: *Most of the United States from the eastern slopes of the Rocky Mountains to the Atlantic, and from the Gulf Coast north to the Great Lakes and extending into southern Ontario and Quebec. Most anglers use them as bait and seldom distinguish them.*

WHERE TO FISH: *Roams widely, but seems to prefer open water over mud bottom.*

DESCRIPTION: Rounder and generally smaller than anadromous Shads. The color is much the same, but a long, thread-like final ray of the dorsal fin easily identifies this one and the upper jaw and snout are rounded.

SIZE: Average length is 4-10 inches. A few top 16 inches. World record 4 pounds, 6 ounces.

FOOD VALUE: None. Only value is as bait.

GAME QUALITIES: Frantic but not strong.

TACKLE: Nets. Seldom caught on a hook.

LURES AND BAITS: None dependable. Occasionally strikes small jigs and live minnows.

Threadfin Shad

Dorosoma petenense

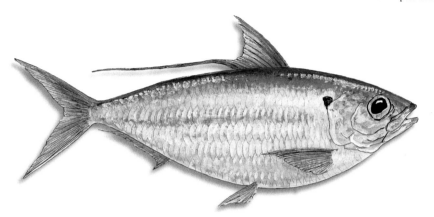

DESCRIPTION: Blue to green on the back, with silvery sides. Has a pointed snout and frontal mouth. Black specks on inside and outside of lower jaw. Eye is large.

SIZE: Seldom more than 6 inches.

FOOD VALUE: None. Only value is as bait.

GAME QUALITIES: None.

TACKLE: Nets. Seldom caught on a hook.

LURES AND BAITS: None dependable.

RANGE: *Most of Florida plus rivers and reservoirs of the Gulf Coast from Florida to Southwest Texas, and in the Mississippi drainage as far north as Indiana; south into Central America. Widely introduced as forage to other areas.*

WHERE TO FISH: *Schools in open water of reservoirs, slow streams and eddies.*

Goldeye

Hiodon alosoides

RANGE: *Widespread in Canada, from coast to coast and far into the Arctic. In the United States, it ranges in the Mississippi system from Louisiana to Minnesota and up the Ohio and Missouri rivers. Also found in lakes and impoundments throughout its range.*

WHERE TO FISH: *Open water of lakes and eddies of rivers.*

DESCRIPTION: Body is deep and compressed. Blue to green above with golden sides. Large mouth with lower jaw extending to rear of eye. Sometimes has a few scattered dark spots on upper sides.

SIZE: Average is less than a pound; tops about 2 pounds. World record 3 pounds, 13 ounces.

FOOD VALUE: Soft and bony but fair smoked.

GAME QUALITIES: Scrappy panfish.

TACKLE: Fly, ultralight spinning, pole.

LURES AND BAITS: Natural insects and dry flies are best. A few are taken on small jigs and spoons.

Mooneye

Hiodon tergisus

DESCRIPTION: Back is green with blue reflection. Body is flattened and silvery. Distinguishing characteristics include smaller mouth than the Goldeye, not extending past eye, large eyes, short snout, and a small flap located just above the pelvic fin. Also has teeth on the tongue and roof of mouth.

SIZE: Slightly larger than the Goldeye, it runs 1-2 pounds on average. World record 1 pound, 3 ounces.

FOOD VALUE: Soft and bony.

GAME QUALITIES: Scrappy but small.

TACKLE: Ultralight spinning and light fly.

LURES AND BAITS: Small jigs and spoons; small dry flies and natural insects.

RANGE: *From the Hudson Bay region of Canada southward through the Ohio Valley into Mississippi. Extends eastward to the Great Lakes (except Superior) and the St. Lawrence Waterway.*

WHERE TO FISH: *Generally prefers clearer water than the Goldeye. Best fishing is in open water when fish are feeding at the surface.*

Rainbow Smelt

Osmerus mordax

OTHER NAMES:

American Smelt
Arctic Smelt
Atlantic Smelt
Pygmy Smelt

RANGE: *In the East, from Michigan to New York and north to Labrador, including all the Great Lakes. In the Pacific, from Vancouver Island to the entire coastal area of Alaska.*

WHERE TO FISH: *Stays close to shore in lakes and enters rivers to spawn. Best fishing is in river mouths. Good action for ice fisherman in rivers and coastal flats. Smelt fries are a popular tradition wherever they're common.*

DESCRIPTION: Green or brown above; silvery sides with pink iridescence. Often has a streak of brighter silver down the side from gill to tail.

SIZE: Averages 8-12 inches, seldom grows much larger.

FOOD VALUE: Excellent, but must be kept well iced.

GAME QUALITIES: Too small for much pull.

TACKLE: Dipnet, pole, ultralight spinning.

LURES AND BAITS: Bits of cut fish, worms or crustaceans; natural insects.

Longfin Smelt

Spirinchus thaleichthys

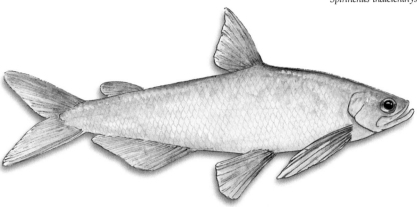

DESCRIPTION: Very large mouth with jaw extending to or beyond eye. Brown or iridescent green above with silvery sides. No streak of darker silver along sides.

SIZE: Seldom exceeds 6 inches.

FOOD VALUE: Excellent.

GAME QUALITIES: Too small to put up much resistance.

TACKLE: Dipnets. Some are caught on tiny silver or gold hooks, baited and unbaited.

LURES AND BAITS: Bits of cut fish, shrimp, or bacon.

OTHER NAMES:

Sacramento Smelt

RANGE: Coastal streams of the Pacific from Central California to southern Alaska. Landlocked in some lakes of Washington State and British Columbia.

WHERE TO FISH: Along shore-lines of bays and river mouths.

What? A Minnow weighing 10 or 20 pounds, or even more? Certainly. The Minnow family is the largest in the North American freshwater fish kingdom and its members vary in size, although most people—anglers and lubbers alike—tend to think of Minnows only as those tiny fish you use for bait, or the little critters that nibble on your goosebumps when you swim in the lake. That popular misconception is understandable, considering that the great majority of Minnows are indeed very small. But again, members of this vast group come in all proportions, from mammoth to microscopic. Behemoths of the family include several species of Carps and also the Colorado Pikeminnow (previously called Squawfish before political correctness dictated a change in nomenclature). Various types of both Pikeminnows and Carp can exceed 50 pounds and sometimes hit 75 or 80. Obviously, fish so large are worthy of angling attention. The Common Carp, in particular, seems to be attracting an ever-growing number of sportsmen, who have found that in addition to traditional doughballs, Carp will also hit properly presented jigs and flies. Still, most of the Minnows are little fellows, but even the types that are only a few inches long often draw hook-and-line attention from youngsters, and also from adults seeking bait. Bait needs are usually much easier to fill, however, with dipnets or seines.

The Minnows

Common Carp

Grass Carp

Bighead Carp

Goldfish

Hardhead

Sacramento Blackfish

Northern Pikeminnow

Sacramento Pikeminnow

Umpqua Pikeminnow

Colorado Pikeminnow

Fallfish

Creek Chub

Lake Chub

Dixie Chub

Humpback Chub

Roundtail Chub

Hornyhead Chub

Bonytail

Peamouth

Emerald Shiner

Golden Shiner

River Shiner

Common Carp

Cyprinus carpio

OTHER NAMES:

German Carp
European Carp
King Carp

RANGE: Not native to America, but now found over most of the United States and southern Canada.

WHERE TO FISH: Hard to pinpoint, since Carp feed deep and shallow, in waters from crystal clear to very murky.

DESCRIPTION: Greenish above with a white belly, and a brassy or golden sheen. The fins are reddish. Has a barbel on each side of the small rubbery mouth.

SIZE: Commonly runs from 2 to 20 pounds, but much bigger fish are sometimes taken. North American record 57 pounds, 13 ounces. World record 75 pounds, 11 ounces, from France.

FOOD VALUE: Not highly regarded but edible. Bony.

GAME QUALITIES: Carp are very strong, bullish fighters. They stay hooked well because of their rubbery mouths, and a big one will take a while to land, even on moderately heavy tackle.

TACKLE: Stout spinning and baitcasting tackle is needed. In some situations, Carp can be taken by fly fishing as well.

LURES AND BAITS: Many natural baits are used, including doughballs and numerous "secret concoctions" of individual anglers. Worms and crayfish are good producers too. About the only productive artificial lures are jigs and sinking flies, worked very slowly.

Grass Carp

Ctenopharyngodon idella

DESCRIPTION: Torpedo shaped. Back is dark green to brown and the belly is white or yellowish. Frontal mouth has no barbels. Scales are large.

SIZE: Averages 5-15 pounds but can grow much larger—at least to 65 pounds. World record 68 pounds, 12 ounces.

FOOD VALUE: Poor.

GAME QUALITIES: Difficult to tempt, but once hooked it puts up a stout if not spectacular battle, typified by long runs and occasional jumps.

TACKLE: Spinning, baitcasting, fly.

LURES AND BAITS: Not a ready biter but can sometimes be taken on doughballs and other Carp baits; also on flies tied to look like the particular type of vegetation on which the Grass Carp are feeding in the area.

OTHER NAMES:

Amur
White Amur

RANGE: *Non-native (Asian) species, Grass Carp have been introduced to control weeds in certain waters of many states. They have spread through the major river systems of the U.S.*

WHERE TO FISH: *Close to shore in weedy areas.*

Bighead Carp

Hypophthalmichthys nobilis

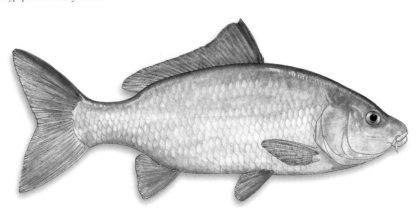

OTHER NAMES:

Bigmouth Carp
Chinese Carp

RANGE: *An Asian species accidentally introduced into the Missouri and Mississippi rivers and also to various other parts of the U.S., including South Florida and California.*

WHERE TO FISH: *Not really fishable, although a rare one may be caught with a hook, and others are sometimes snagged by fishermen seeking Paddlefish in Midwest rivers. These Carp often school with Paddlefish.*

DESCRIPTION: Head is very large and mouth wide. Tail is forked. Color is dusky green on back; pale on sides and belly. Some specimens are nearly white, while others are marbled.

SIZE: Reportedly can grow to at least 60 pounds. World record 47 pounds.

FOOD VALUE: Very good but little tested in the U.S.

GAME QUALITIES: Strong battler when hooked.

TACKLE: None effective.

LURES AND BAITS: Bigmouth Carp are plankton feeders that take a baited hook only accidentally.

Goldfish

Carassius auratus

DESCRIPTION: The gold and multi-colored hues seen in aquarium Goldfish are seldom present in wild ones, whose color is brown or brassy on the sides and green to brown on the dorsal surface. The body is deep and the mouth small. Dorsal and anal fins are large.

SIZE: From a few ounces to more than 5 pounds. World record 6 pounds, 10 ounces.

FOOD VALUE: Not often eaten.

GAME QUALITIES: Scrappy but small.

TACKLE: Pole.

LURES AND BAITS: Takes many natural baits—earthworms and larvae, cheese, doughballs and corn, to name a few.

RANGE: Non-native, the Goldfish has long since been introduced to waters throughout the United States and southern Canada—sometimes deliberately but more often accidentally, either by release of pet fish or by using Goldfish as bait.

WHERE TO FISH: Shallow, mud-bottomed waters of warm ponds, lakes or slow-moving streams.

Hardhead

Mylopharodon conocephalus

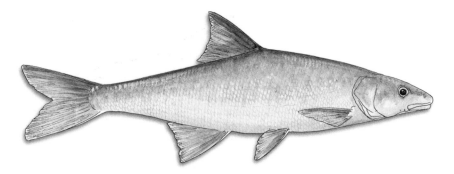

OTHER NAMES:

California Hardhead

RANGE: *Sacramento, San Joaquin and Russian River drainages and Pit River system, California.*

WHERE TO FISH: *On bottom in deep pools. Not often sought.*

DESCRIPTION: Body is long and slender with a long, pointed snout. Color is brown above, silver on the sides.

SIZE: Another large minnow, it can exceed 2 feet in length, though the usual size is 12-15 inches.

FOOD VALUE: Good.

GAME QUALITIES: Fair when large.

TACKLE: Pole, spinning gear.

LURES AND BAITS: Not much for lures but takes more kinds of bait than the Blackfish. Worms, insects, cut baits and shellfish often do well.

Sacramento Blackfish

Orthodon microlepidotus

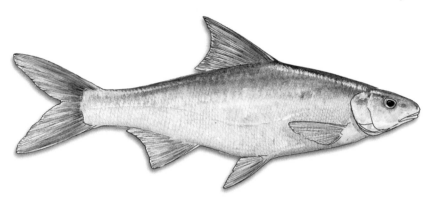

DESCRIPTION: Head is wide and flat and the mouth slightly upturned. Body is slender and the body just forward of the tail is long and narrow. Color is gray-green above with silvery sides.

SIZE: Averages about 8 inches; occasionally grows to 2 feet.

FOOD VALUE: Good.

GAME QUALITIES: Fair.

TACKLE: Pole or spinning outfit.

LURES AND BAITS: A grazer, it will suck up small baits fished on or near bottom, in the manner of Mullet. Worms, bread crusts and bits of bacon are among baits used.

RANGE: Sacramento-San Joaquin river systems, Clear Lake, Pajaro River and Salinas River.

WHERE TO FISH: On bottom in still water. Not often targeted by anglers.

Northern Pikeminnow

Ptychocheilus oregonensis

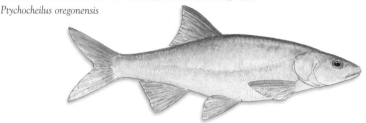

OTHER NAMES:

Northern Squawfish
Columbia
  Pikeminnow
Common
  Pikeminnow

RANGE: *Columbia River basin and other coastal drainages of Oregon and Washington, but range extends northward to British Columbia.*

WHERE TO FISH: *Deep holes, rocky pools and below dams, especially on the Columbia.*

DESCRIPTION: Color is similar to other Pikeminnows, but anglers can easily differentiate among them by geography alone.

SIZE: Smaller than the Colorado species, it typically runs 1-3 pounds, but reportedly can exceed 20 pounds.

FOOD VALUE: Poor.

GAME QUALITIES: Mediocre; not powerful or spectacular.

TACKLE: Spinning and baitcasting gear.

LURES AND BAITS: Live minnows and all minnow-imitating lures can be effective, including spoons and diving plugs.

Sacramento Pikeminnow

Ptychocheilus grandis

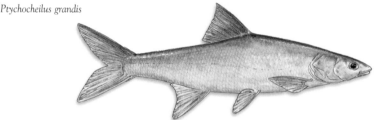

OTHER NAMES:

Sacramento
  Squawfish

RANGE: *Distributed throughout the Sacramento-San Joaquin river system and also in the Pajaro, Salinas, Russian and upper Pit rivers.*

WHERE TO FISH: *Lower reaches of tributaries and open water of estuaries; also large lakes.*

DESCRIPTION: Similar in color to related Pikeminnows— blue-green to gray above and silvery below. Scientists separate them by means of scales and ray counts. Anglers simply rely on geography.

SIZE: Most run 1 or 2 pounds; largest on record is 14.5 pounds.

FOOD VALUE: Poor.

GAME QUALITIES: Mediocre.

TACKLE: Light spinning or pole.

LURES AND BAITS: Worms, insects and minnows. Small spinners, plastic worms and spoons.

Umpqua Pikeminnow

Ptychocheilus umpquae

DESCRIPTION: Very similar to the Northern Pikeminnow, except scales are smaller.

SIZE: Smallest of the Pikeminnows; seldom exceeds a couple of pounds.

FOOD VALUE: Poor.

GAME QUALITIES: So-so.

TACKLE: Spinning and baitcasting gear.

LURES AND BAITS: Live minnows and all minnow-imitating lures can be effective, including spoons and diving plugs.

OTHER NAMES:

Umpqua Squawfish

RANGE: Umpqua and Siuslaw rivers and their tributaries in Oregon, and some lakes of that area.

WHERE TO FISH: Not often sought, but likes eddies and backwaters and quiet, deep holes.

Colorado Pikeminnow

Ptychocheilus lucius

DESCRIPTION: The body is compressed and the head takes nearly a fourth of its entire length. Dorsal and ventral fins are set well to the rear. Tail is forked. Color is gray-blue above, silvery below.

SIZE: Largest Pikeminnow, one reportedly reached 5 feet and a weight of more than 50 pounds.

FOOD VALUE: Poor.

GAME QUALITIES: Powerful fighter.

TACKLE: The full range of casting gear.

LURES AND BAITS: Both predatory and omnivorous, it will take all sorts of fish and insect baits, as well as many artificial lures.

OTHER NAMES:

Colorado Squawfish

RANGE: Primarily the Colorado River basin.

WHERE TO FISH: Deep rocky or sandy pools. Once on the endangered list, it now is increasing but still holds threatened status and fishing is discouraged.

Fallfish

Semotilus corporalis

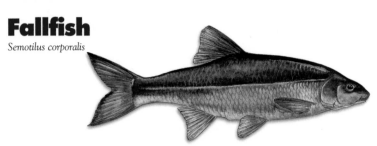

OTHER NAMES:

Chub
Eastern Chub

RANGE: *Atlantic States from North Carolina northward, and southeastern Canada.*

WHERE TO FISH: *Larger specimens favor deep pools in small to midsize streams. Small fish school in shallows near shore.*

DESCRIPTION: Similar to the Creek Chub but lacks dark spot on dorsal fin. Round snout overhangs the mouth. Large scales and eyes. Color is brown above with large silvery sides that sometimes show a purple sheen.

SIZE: Larger than the Creek Chub, it averages 10 inches and commonly exceeds 12 inches. World record 3 pounds, 8 ounces.

FOOD VALUE: Poor (bait value excellent).

GAME QUALITIES: Scruffy battler for its size.

TACKLE: Fly rods (sometimes a great nuisance to fly fishermen), pole, nets.

LURES AND BAITS: Hits many small flies and hard artificials such as spinners. Worms and any sort of insect baits are productive.

Creek Chub

Semotilus atromaculatus

RANGE: *Most of the eastern United States from Central Georgia to southeastern Canada.*

WHERE TO FISH: *Rocky and sandy pools and runs in creeks and small rivers.*

DESCRIPTION: Olive brown above with a dark stripe along side. Breeding males sport orange and pink around dorsal fin and lower sides and bumps on the snout, called nuptial tubercles. Dark spot at the base of dorsal fin. Mouth is large, extending beyond eye.

SIZE: Averages 4-6 inches; occasionally to 10 inches.

FOOD VALUE: Poor. Main value is for forage and bait for riverine gamefishes.

GAME QUALITIES: Too small to resist much.

TACKLE: Pole (seldom fished for except by youngsters); also seines and dipnets when seeking bait.

LURES AND BAITS: Worms, insects, doughballs. Often takes wet flies intended for Trout.

Lake Chub

Couesius plumbeus

DESCRIPTION: Brown to dark green above, with white or silvery undersides. Dark band often present on sides. Tiny barbel under mouth.

SIZE: A large Chub, it averages 6 inches in length and can reach 9 or 10 inches.

FOOD VALUE: Pretty good, but bony.

GAME QUALITIES: Usually a willing biter and a fair battler for its size.

TACKLE: Pole or light spinning gear. Caught on sinking flies but usually by accident.

LURES AND BAITS: Takes nearly any small bait or insect.

RANGE: Most of Canada in the U.S., it occurs south to New York, the Great Lakes region, the Platte River, Colorado, and the Columbia River drainage in Washington.

WHERE TO FISH: Most familiar along shallow rocky shorelines of lakes, but also found in pools of slow streams.

Dixie Chub

Semotilus thoreauianus

DESCRIPTION: Dark olive to black back with numerous tiny light dots. Underside is white.

SIZE: Up to 6 inches.

FOOD VALUE: Minimal.

GAME QUALITIES: Minimal. Often sought for bait for stream Bass.

TACKLE: Minnow seine or pole.

LURES AND BAITS: Bits of earthworm.

RANGE: Ochlockonee River system in Georgia and Florida, west to Tombigbee River system in Alabama.

WHERE TO FISH: Small rivers and creeks, in deep, sandy pools.

Humpback Chub
Gila cypha

RANGE: Upper and middle reaches of the Colorado and Green rivers in Wyoming, Colorado, Utah and Arizona. Scarce everywhere, but most abundant near mouth of Little Colorado River, Arizona.

WHERE TO FISH: Not fished for deliberately. Likes fast runs and flowing pools.

DESCRIPTION: Color is silvery, with prominent black lateral line. Pectoral and anal fins brown to reddish. The huge hump forces water down on the flat head so the fish can maintain position in strong current.

SIZE: Usually 4-6 inches; maximum perhaps 10 inches.

FOOD VALUE: Insignificant.

GAME QUALITIES: Poor.

TACKLE: Accidental catch, usually on trout or panfish tackle.

LURES AND BAITS: Sinking flies or small worms and insects.

Roundtail Chub
Gila robusta

RANGE: Colorado River drainage in Wyoming, Colorado, Utah, Nevada, New Mexico and Arizona.

WHERE TO FISH: Although it prefers moving water over sand or rock bottom, it is common in a number of western impoundments.

DESCRIPTION: Overall gold or silvery sheen with small and irregular black dots. Tail is deeply forked and lobes rounded. High dorsal and anal fins also have rounded tips.

SIZE: Often exceeds 1 foot in length.

FOOD VALUE: Not bad, but bony.

GAME QUALITIES: Has the heft to resist light tackle with vigor.

TACKLE: Pole, ultralight spinning or light fly gear.

LURES AND BAITS: Takes worms, minnows and small artificials, including wet flies and nymphs.

Hornyhead Chub
Nocomis biguttatus

DESCRIPTION: Very colorful fish. Stout bronze body with iridescent sides. Large red spot located behind eye of male. Fins are yellow or orange. Large tubercles on head.

SIZE: Up to about 10 inches.

FOOD VALUE: Poor.

GAME QUALITIES: Spunky but small.

TACKLE: Often taken incidentally on light spinning and fly gear but any deliberate fishing is usually by children with poles.

LURES AND BAITS: Worms, small crayfish (or pieces); any small insect bait. Hits a variety of small artificial flies.

OTHER NAMES:

Stoneroller

RANGE: *Widely distributed from western New York through the Great Lakes region and the upper Mississippi drainage. Also in the Ozarks and some Rocky Mountain areas.*

WHERE TO FISH: *Prefers small, clear streams with gravel bottom. Not plentiful in large rivers or lakes.*

Bonytail
Gila elegans

DESCRIPTION: Hump is not so pronounced as in Humpback Chub. Upper body brown to dark blue or gray; underparts yellowish or orange; fins red. Forked tail and hard, bony caudal peduncle.

SIZE: To about 18 inches.

FOOD VALUE: Poor.

GAME QUALITIES: Fair.

TACKLE: Not fished for deliberately; sometimes taken on trout or panfish gear.

LURES AND BAITS: Worms and insects; occasionally wet flies.

RANGE: *Colorado River of Wyoming, Colorado, Utah, New Mexico, Arizona, California and Mexico. Rare everywhere except Green River, Utah and some large impoundments of the Colorado River.*

WHERE TO FISH: *Prefers flowing pools and backwaters over mud or rock.*

Emerald Shiner

Notropis atherinoides

OTHER NAMES:

Lake Shiner
Plains Shiner

RANGE: *Distributed over most of the heartland, from the Gulf of Mexico far into the Canadian North, and eastward through the Great Lakes.*

WHERE TO FISH: *Likes clear, open water, regardless of bottom type. Schools at mid-depth and at the surface of lakes and rivers.*

DESCRIPTION: Color is silvery, with a dark stripe that has emerald reflections. The body is rather flat and the dorsal fin is transparent.

SIZE: Averages 4 inches.

FOOD VALUE: None. Bait value high.

GAME QUALITIES: None.

TACKLE: Nets.

LURES AND BAITS: Occasionally (and accidentally) caught on small flies.

Peamouth

Mylocheilus caurinus

OTHER NAMES:

Peamouth Chub
Northwest Dace

RANGE: *Native to the rivers and lakes of northwestern North America as far east as Alberta.*

WHERE TO FISH: *Lakes and slow-moving portions of streams. Concentrates around aquatic vegetation.*

DESCRIPTION: Slender shape. Color is dark brown above, white or silver on sides, with two dark stripes—the lower one shorter than the upper.

SIZE: Averages 6-8 inches. Sometimes reaches or exceeds 12 inches.

FOOD VALUE: Edible but used mostly for bait.

GAME QUALITIES: Poor.

TACKLE: Pole or light spinning gear. Taken incidentally on fly tackle.

LURES AND BAITS: Worms or small aquatic insects. Small artificial flies.

Golden Shiner

Notemigonus crysoleucas

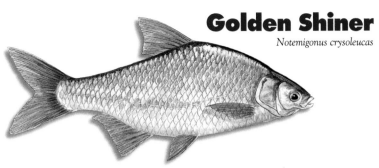

DESCRIPTION: Broad-bodied shiner with large scales that usually flash gold but may be silver in clear water. Reddish fins. Small head with upturned mouth. Forked tail.

SIZE: From a couple of inches to more than 12 inches.

FOOD VALUE: Poor; but bait value is high.

GAME QUALITIES: Not much pull but great enjoyment for many youngsters, who find them easy to catch, particularly after the area has been chummed with oatmeal or bread crumbs.

TACKLE: Pole or, for bait, cast nets (check local laws).

LURES AND BAITS: Bits of worm, or doughballs.

OTHER NAMES:

**Roach
Bitterhead Chub**

RANGE: *Native to most of the United States and southern Canada east of the Rockies. Transplanted widely in the West as well—mostly by the bait business.*

WHERE TO FISH: *Shiners are found in all kinds of water from large lakes to tiny streams. They generally stick close to thick grass, lily pads, or other aquatic vegetation.*

River Shiner

Notropis blennius

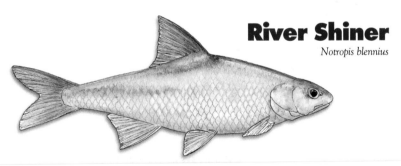

DESCRIPTION: Body is slender and slightly compressed. Overall color is tan to light green above with silver sides and a dark stripe along the back that encircles the dorsal fin. Stripe also seen on the rear portion of the side.

SIZE: Average length 2-3 inches.

FOOD VALUE: None. Bait value high.

GAME QUALITIES: None.

TACKLE: Nets.

LURES AND BAITS: Seldom caught on a hook.

RANGE: *Hudson Bay drainage from Alberta to Manitoba, and through the Mississippi River drainage to Texas and Louisiana.*

WHERE TO FISH: *Schools in largest rivers and lower portions of main tributaries, usually over sand or gravel bottom.*

Sculpins comprise a very large family of bottom-dwelling fishes that live in the seas as well as in fresh water. Some marine species are reasonably large and are pursued by bottom fishermen for fun and food. The freshwater species are all little guys that live, for the most part, in streams, generally hiding under rocks and making themselves as invisible as possible. Anglers are not likely to realize they are present, unless they happen to find one clinging to a fly intended for Trout. Observant fly fishermen realized long ago that these little fish are a very popular item on the menu of Trout, especially big Trout, and so they developed a family of large flies, called muddlers, that are designed to imitate Sculpins. For that reason alone, Sculpins are important figures in the angling world, because muddlers are among the standard tools of fly fishermen, who use them effectively for Bass and other species. The Sculpins covered in this chapter represent numerous similar species that abound throughout the continent. The last fish in this chapter—the Round Goby—is a special case, and not a happy one. It is a native of the Middle East that was introduced to the Great Lakes by accident. Now in all five of the lakes, it is reproducing rapidly and is a threat to the well-being of native species.

Sculpins and Gobies

Mottled Sculpin
Slimy Sculpin
Fourhorn Sculpin
Round Goby

Mottled Sculpin

Cottus bairdi

OTHER NAMES:

Columbia Sculpin
Miller's Thumb
Gudgeon

RANGE: *Covers most of the northern United States and much of eastern Canada. In the West, it inhabits the Mountain States from Washington to Colorado. In Canada it ranges from Saskatchewan to eastern Quebec and north to the Arctic regions of Hudson Bay. Isolated populations occur in the Ozarks and New Mexico.*

WHERE TO FISH: *Likes riffles of small streams, but also found along lake edges.*

DESCRIPTION: Flattened head. Tan to dark brown above, with dark brown mottling and two or three dark bars on sides. Chin is speckled. Dorsal fin has orange edge.

SIZE: Averages 3 inches; up to 6 inches.

FOOD VALUE: None, but it makes good bait.

GAME QUALITIES: None.

TACKLE: Not targeted but can be caught with poles; also hits small wet flies on occasion, usually to the distress of the fisherman.

LURES AND BAITS: Any sort of insect or pieces of worm. Will also take flies.

Slimy Sculpin

Cottus cognatus

OTHER NAMES:

Slimy Mudder
Northern Sculpin

RANGE: *Widely distributed throughout Canada and Alaska. In the Lower 48 States, it is found in the northern Rockies, the Great Lakes States and East Coast States from Maine south to Virginia.*

WHERE TO FISH: *Cool-water riffles of streams and rocky portions of lakes.*

DESCRIPTION: Color is dark brown above, lighter below, with mottled upper sides and back. "Thorns" are on head and at base of pectoral fins. Dark blotch at base of second dorsal fin.

SIZE: Averages around 2-3 inches; 5 is about the longest.

FOOD VALUE: None, but is a prime forage species for Trout and other gamefish.

GAME QUALITIES: None.

TACKLE: Not often fished for, but taken incidentally on flies and small spinning lures.

LURES AND BAITS: Feeds on variety of aquatic insect and crustacean life, and tiny minnows.

Fourhorn Sculpin

Myoxocephalus quadricornis

DESCRIPTION: Brown back and sides with white belly. Greenish mottling on sides and green saddles across back. Head is flat and wide with large mouth. Two "horns" between the eyes and two more at rear of head.

SIZE: Usually around 4 inches; grows to about 10 inches.

FOOD VALUE: Poor.

GAME QUALITIES: Poor.

TACKLE: Seldom sought but can be caught on fly or spinning gear.

LURES AND BAITS: Minnows, worms, artificial flies and spinners.

OTHER NAMES:

Scorpion Fish

RANGE: *Circumpolar distribution in both fresh water and marine environments of the northern extremes.*

WHERE TO FISH: *Not targeted but can be caught near shore in both streams and lakes. Valuable bait for Lake Trout and Burbot.*

Round Goby

Neogobius melanostomus

DESCRIPTION: Color is tan or brown with black mottling on sides and back. Eyes are large and protruding. Single black spot on rear edge of forward dorsal fin is a distinguishing mark. Has only a single pelvic fin. Pectoral and caudal fins are large and rounded.

SIZE: Averages around 5 inches; can reach 10 inches or slightly more.

FOOD VALUE: Edible but unappetizing.

GAME QUALITIES: Poor.

TACKLE: A nuisance species ignored by anglers, it can nevertheless be caught with pole or any light tackle.

LURES AND BAITS: Wide appetite includes exotic zebra mussels, aquatic insects and small fish. Strikes boldly at many artificial lures.

RANGE: *An accidental introduction from the Black and Caspian seas, it now is established in all the Great Lakes and threatens to expand, with possible dire results for some native species.*

WHERE TO FISH: *Prefers rocky areas but also inhabits sandbars.*

Minnows in appearance but not in name, these Silversides and Livebearers are representatives of large groups that are familiar in most waters from coast to coast and from Canada to the Gulf of Mexico. Only a few can be taken by hook and line, and even those fall prey mostly to children with tiny hooks. They remain fixtures in the sportfishing world, however, because of their value as bait. The larger ones take many Bass, Walleye and Trout, while the smaller specimens do deadly work on such types as Crappie, White Bass and Yellow Perch. The Killifishes and Sheepshead Minnow abound in the lower reaches of most streams along the Atlantic and Gulf shores, and they make fine bait for both freshwater and saltwater species, which frequently mingle in tidal waters (see Chapter 10). Killifish, Sheepshead Minnows and others that hang out in shallow, weedy areas are easily taken with minnow traps. Catching the open-water types for bait may require a cast net, but check with local regulations.

Silversides and Livebearers

Brook Silverside

Atlantic Silverside

Inland Silverside

Sailfin Molly

Banded Killifish

Mummichog

Sheepshead Minnow

Brook Silverside

Labidesthes sicculus

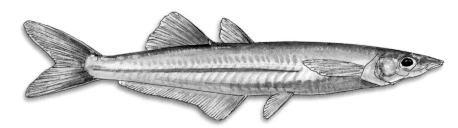

OTHER NAMES:

Silverside

RANGE: *Streams and lakes in Atlantic and Gulf drainages from South Carolina to Texas; also Mississippi River basins from Louisiana to Minnesota and eastward to the Great Lakes and Quebec. Widely introduced elsewhere as forage for game species.*

WHERE TO FISH: *Schools usually in open water, anywhere from near shore to middle reaches.*

DESCRIPTION: Slender, translucent body; pale green with a silver stripe along the side. Snout is long, and anal fin is long and sickle-shaped.

SIZE: Average length 3 inches; maximum about 5 inches.

FOOD VALUE: None, but it makes good bait.

GAME QUALITIES: None.

TACKLE: Nets.

LURES AND BAITS: None.

Atlantic Silverside

Menidia menidia

DESCRIPTION: Color is olive above and white below, with a silver streak from gill to tail and numerous tiny dots. Mouth is very small.

SIZE: Averages 2-4 inches; may reach 6 inches.

FOOD VALUE: Good, but seldom eaten.

GAME QUALITIES: None.

TACKLE: Nets. Not taken on hook and line.

LURES AND BAITS: None.

OTHER NAMES:

Sand Smelt
Spearing

RANGE: Gulf of St. Lawrence to Florida East Coast.

WHERE TO FISH: Usually found along seashores and river mouths, but sometimes enters fresh water, especially the St. Johns River, Florida, and streams entering Chesapeake Bay.

Inland Silverside

Menidia beryllina

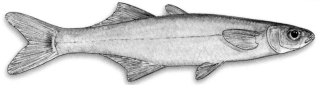

DESCRIPTION: Flattened head. A silver stripe extends from the gill cover to the caudal fin.

SIZE: Average 3 to 4 inches.

FOOD VALUE: Good but seldom eaten.

GAME QUALITIES: None.

TACKLE: Nets.

LURES AND BAITS: None.

OTHER NAMES:

Tidewater
Silverside

RANGE: Widely distributed from Massachusetts around Florida to Mexico, and is common both along the coast and far inland, especially in the Mississippi River where it extends north to Illinois.

WHERE TO FISH: Silversides school in open water.

Sailfin Molly

Poecilia latipinna

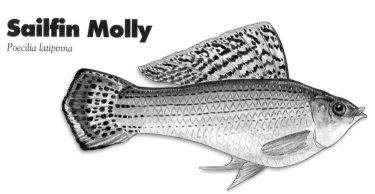

RANGE: *Atlantic and Gulf drainages from North Carolina to Mexico. Introduced to the Colorado River drainage, Arizona, and scattered other waters.*

WHERE TO FISH: *Ponds, marshes and quiet streams, usually around vegetation and easy to spot near the surface.*

DESCRIPTION: Male has very large and sail-like dorsal fin, with black spots on outer half and orange trim. Color is greenish above and yellowish below, with several rows of dark spots. Some individuals vividly marked with orange. Flat head and upturned mouth.

SIZE: To about 6 inches.

FOOD VALUE: None. Bait value good, especially for Crappie and Sunfish. Also prized as aquarium pets.

GAME QUALITIES: None.

TACKLE: Dipnets, traps.

LURES AND BAITS: None.

Banded Killifish

Fundulus diaphanus

OTHER NAMES:

Killie

RANGE: *Coastal drainages from Newfoundland to South Carolina; also the Great Lakes and Mississippi drainages from Canada south to Pennsylvania and west to the Dakotas.*

WHERE TO FISH: *Marginal areas of lakes, ponds and slow streams, usually around vegetation.*

DESCRIPTION: It has a long, slim body banded with several dark bars on silver sides. Color is tan to brown above with a dark stripe along back. Yellowish below. Rounded caudal fin.

SIZE: Usually 2-5 inches.

FOOD VALUE: None. Bait value good.

GAME QUALITIES: None.

TACKLE: Can be caught with pole and tiny hooks, but gathered for bait more efficiently with dipnets.

LURES AND BAITS: Doughballs, bits of bacon, or earthworms.

Mummichog

Fundulus heteroclitus

DESCRIPTION: Fat body and blunt head make its appearance unlike other Killifishes, but it is one of the best known. It has a fanlike tail and dorsal fin. Color usually is mottled brown, often with stripes.

SIZE: Most run 2-4 inches; maximum about 6 inches.

FOOD VALUE: Poor. Bait value very good.

GAME QUALITIES: Fun for youngsters.

TACKLE: Can be caught with poles, but bait-seekers prefer nets or traps.

LURES AND BAITS: Any sort of small cut bait—fish, worms or crustacean.

OTHER NAMES:

Mud Minnow
Marsh Minnow
Killifish

RANGE: *Atlantic drainages from Labrador to Florida. Usually in salty or brackish water, but enters fresh water.*

WHERE TO FISH: *Muddy flats near shore.*

Sheepshead Minnow

Cyprinodon variegatus

DESCRIPTION: Deep-bodied and Sunfish-shaped with rounded tail. Color is gray above and silvery on sides, with dark vertical bars.

SIZE: Usually 1-2 inches; may reach 3 inches.

FOOD VALUE: None, but bait value is high.

GAME QUALITIES: None.

TACKLE: Dipnet or minnow trap.

LURES AND BAITS: None.

OTHER NAMES:

Variegated
Minnow
Mud Minnow

RANGE: *All East Coast and Gulf Coast states, both in salt marshes and nearby fresh water. Some freshwater populations are isolated.*

WHERE TO FISH: *Shallow water with sandy or silty bottom and little vegetation.*

Index

In-Fisherman Books

IN-FISHERMAN MASTERPIECE SERIES

- **WALLEYE WISDOM:** A Handbook of Strategies
- **PIKE:** A Handbook of Strategies
- **SMALLMOUTH BASS:** A Handbook of Strategies
- **CRAPPIE WISDOM:** A Handbook of Strategies
- **CHANNEL CATFISH FEVER:** A Handbook of Strategies
- **LARGEMOUTH BASS IN THE 90s:** A Handbook of Strategies
- **BIG BASS MAGIC**
- **FISHING FUNDAMENTALS**
- **ICE FISHING SECRETS**

Each masterpiece book represents the collaborative effort of fishing experts. The books don't represent a regional perspective or the opinions of just one angler. Each masterpiece book teems with information applicable to all areas of the country and to any fishing situation.